URBANIZING AMERICA

The Development of Cities in the
United States from the First
European Settlements to 1920

By
Ivan D. Steen

AN ANVIL ORIGINAL
Under the general editorship of
Hans L. Trefousse

KRIEGER PUBLISHING COMPANY
MALABAR, FLORIDA
2006

THE ANVIL SERIES

Anvil paperbacks give an original analysis of a major field of history or a problem area, drawing upon the most recent research. They present a concise treatment and can act as supplementary material for college history courses. Written by many of the outstanding historians in the United States, the format is one-half narrative text, one-half supporting documents, often from hard to find sources.

Original Edition 2006

Printed and Published by
KRIEGER PUBLISHING COMPANY
KRIEGER DRIVE
MALABAR, FLORIDA 32950

FROM A DECLARATION OF PRINCIPLES JOINTLY ADOPTED BY A COMMITTEE OF THE AMERICAN BAR ASSOCIATION AND A COMMITTEE OF PUBLISHERS:
This publication is designed to provide accurate and authoritative information in regard to the subject matter covered. It is sold with the understanding that the publisher is not engaged in rendering legal, accounting, or other professional service. If legal advice or other expert assistance is required, the services of a competent professional person should be sought.

Library of Congress Cataloging-in-Publication Data

Steen, Ivan D., 1936–
    Urbanizing America : the development of cities in the United States from the first European settlements to 1920 / by Ivan D, Steen.
        p. cm. — (Anvil series (Huntington, N.Y.))
    "An Anvil original".
    Includes bibliographical references and index.
    ISBN 1-57524-165-X (pbk. : alk. paper)
        1. Urbanization—United States—History. 2. Cities and towns—United States—Growth. I. Title. II. Series.

HT384.U5S74   2006
307.760973—dc22   2006040948

10 9 8 7 6 5 4 3 2

CONTENTS

INTRODUCTION

When the Census Bureau completed its count of the residents of the United States in 1920 the resulting compilation revealed that, for the first time, more than half of all Americans were living in what were defined as urban places. The United States was now an urban nation. Of course, this shift took place some time between the censuses of 1910 and 1920, and the change took place over a long period of time. Yet, even while the nation had been primarily rural, the urban sector wielded an influence that was disproportionate to the numbers it represented. The economic, political, social, and cultural impact of the cities was significant in shaping the nation. This was true from the earliest settlement by Europeans in what they saw as a "new world." As settlement moved westward on the North American continent new cities continually were established. Cities were essential to the American economy, serving as centers for the reception and distribution of agricultural products, and later as the locations for manufacturing enterprise. These economic activities were so essential to the growth and survival of the cities that they engaged in a vigorous competition for raw materials and markets. That competition led to the development of much of the transportation network during the nineteenth century, which involved some amazing engineering feats.

Economic gain, in one way or another, also was the principal driving force in the movement of populations. The earliest European settlers came to America primarily because of the promise of economic betterment, and many saw cities as offering the greatest potential to achieve it. The subsequent migration of Europeans and others to the United States also was guided primarily by the hope of economic gain. The rapidly growing cities offered ready employment for these people, along with the hope of improving their status. Not only immigrants, but also Americans of longer standing saw cities as places of opportunity. New cities being established in western regions appeared especially attractive, and some of them enjoyed phenomenal growth.

The crowding together of great numbers of people in these rapidly growing cities created many problems that needed to be addressed by municipal governments. Some of these were physical, such as providing for water, laying out and maintaining streets, and fighting fires; while others were more social in nature, such as providing poor relief, ensuring adequate housing, dealing with crime, and grappling with issues concerning health and sanitation. The greatest obstacle in the way of launching successful attacks on these problems was the prevailing belief that governments should do as little as possible; rather, individuals should look out for themselves. It was soon realized, however, that in an urban environment there were many areas in which self-help was insufficient. In those circumstances, community action was needed, and this was accomplished through voluntarism. But, since people often avoid volunteering, service often was required. Many essential services also were provided by private companies that expected to make a profit. It was only when private effort proved to be inadequate that municipal governments stepped in. And so the failure of the private sector to provide for an acceptable level of service at a reasonable price resulted in city governments gradually taking on more and more functions.

Americans also were reluctant to have their city governments pass laws that would regulate their lives in any way. Some restrictions on individuals were accepted, especially laws that were concerned with protection from fire. But in other areas progress came slowly, and city ordinances and other actions frequently were instituted only after major disasters occurred. Thus, police organization was achieved only after the inadequacy of the existing system was demonstrated in a series of major riots, and sanitary regulations were instituted only after devastating epidemics. Housing regulations were even slower to be enacted, since there was significant resistance to the idea of telling people what they could do with the property they owned.

Not only were American cities gradually changing by taking on new functions, they also significantly were changing in appearance. They changed in density and area, but they also changed in height. The need to house more people and businesses in a relatively limited area led to an increase in the height of buildings, which was facilitated by several technological developments. Thus, American cities have come to be characterized by their tall buildings.

The goal of this volume is to provide an overview of these issues and many others, and thereby provide its readers with an understanding of how the United States became an urban nation. The included documents were chosen mostly to provide contemporary commentary on various aspects of America's cities over a period of nearly three hundred years.

PART I

URBANIZING AMERICA

CHAPTER 1

THE CITIES OF COLONIAL AMERICA

Few of the residents of the colonies that were later to become the United States lived in cities. The first Census of the United States, taken in 1790, classified only one in twenty Americans as urban dwellers. Yet the small number of colonial cities, with a combined population that never exceeded 10 percent of the total for the thirteen colonies, exerted a profound influence on all facets of colonial life.

Cities and towns are as old as America, usually predating actual settlement. From the very outset the planners of most of the colonies recognized the necessity of their establishment. Indeed, the mercantilist economic system of the time could not function effectively without them. Under that system, colonies existed for the benefit of the mother country. Ideally, colonies would produce wealth in the form of precious metals, especially gold; but lacking that, as was the case with the colonies on the Atlantic coast of North America, they would produce raw materials that were desired by the mother country. The mother country, in turn, would process those materials for domestic consumption, or export to other countries, or back to the colonies. Towns and cities would serve as the focus for this trade in the colonies. Thus, the locations of the earliest towns in each colony were dictated by commercial considerations. Each of the colonial towns, then, was a seaport.

The existence of towns also was dictated by other necessities. Clearly, the new colonies would have to be administered in the New World, and so towns were necessary as governmental centers. And even if the planners had not provided for the establishment of towns, they would have sprung up anyhow. The first European settlers arriving on the strange and potentially inhospitable shores of America, undoubtedly would have gathered together for protection and companionship.

There were many small towns in the American colonies, but only five places achieved populations large enough to be considered cities. Those five cities were Boston, Newport, New York (originally New Amsterdam), Philadelphia, and Charles Town (later Charleston). In 1690 the largest of these was Boston, with a population of approximately 7,000, followed by Philadelphia with 4,000, New York with 3,900, Newport with 2,600, and Charles Town with 1,100. By 1742 Boston's population had increased to more than 16,000, Philadelphia to 13,000, New York to 11,000, Charles Town to 6,800, and Newport to 6,200. An important shift took place by 1760, when Boston slipped to third place behind Philadelphia and New York. In that year, Philadelphia contained nearly 24,000 residents, New York 18,000, Boston 15,600, Charles Town 8,000, and Newport 7,500. From the standpoint of the twenty-first century these would appear to be very small places, but this was the eighteenth century, and as late as 1800 only 3 percent of the world's population lived in cities with populations greater than 5,000. Furthermore, Philadelphia, with an estimated population of 30,000 at the beginning of the American Revolution, was the second-largest city in the British Empire, surpassed only by London.

While several reasons might be given for Boston's loss of first place in population, one of the most important has to do with geography. Because these were all commercial cities, location was a prime factor. While Boston had an excellent harbor, both New York and Philadelphia were more advantageously located for both domestic and foreign trade. Not only were transatlantic and coastal trade routes important, but a city had to be well supplied with goods for that trade, as well as have nearby markets for imports. Here is where a city's hinterland became especially important. In the earliest years this was of less significance, but with the growth of the colonies it took on increasing importance; and both New York and Philadelphia had more extensive and more accessible hinterlands than did Boston.

Appearance. At first glance, these seventeenth- and eighteenth-century cities would appear to have little in common with cities of today. The streets were narrow and often unpaved. The buildings were small and commonly built of wood, especially in the seventeenth century, although by the eighteenth century some stone and brick structures began to be erected. None of these buildings was very tall, and the skylines, such as they were, were dominated by church steeples. Few structures made any concessions to architecture until the eighteenth century, when the cities became more settled. Not surprisingly, most designs were based on British models, although they usually were adapted to suit American conditions and materials. Nonetheless, these colonial cities were very busy places. The streets were crowded with people and various types of vehicles. At the same time, the lines between urban and rural were not as sharply drawn as they are today. In addition to horses, cows, pigs, chickens, and geese were common sights in city streets. Farming and the raising of animals were not unusual occupations for city dwellers.

Boston's narrow, crooked streets seemed to follow no rational plan, giving rise to a belief that they were laid out by a cow. But more than likely they followed paths taken by the city's residents as they took routes around minor topographical variations that are no longer apparent. Soon after its founding, Boston already was taking on urban attributes, with houses built close to each other along streets, many of which were paved. In the eighteenth century some attractive public buildings were erected, most notably Faneuil Hall and King's Chapel. Joined to the mainland by only a narrow strip of land, Bostonians soon began building out into the harbor to accommodate expansion. (*See Document No. 1.*)

Newport was much less urban in appearance than Boston. Houses, instead of being lined up near each other, stood alone on separate plots. Yet while Newport ranked fifth among the colonial cities in population, its buildings were among the most beautiful. This primarily was a result of Newport being the residence of Peter Harrison, the only professional architect in the colonies. He is best known for his designs of the Redwood Library and of a synagogue for Newport's Jewish residents.

New York began its urban existence as New Amsterdam, a colony founded by the Dutch West India Company. Most of the first permanent settlers, however, were not Dutch; rather, they were people known as Walloons, who were Protestants from Belgium. They brought with them detailed instructions from the Dutch West India Company on how to lay out the town. That plan called for a neatly laid out town surrounded by a five-pointed fortification, with long, narrow farms behind the fortification. But this plan was never implemented, and New Amsterdam grew without one. As in Boston, streets developed along paths taken by people and animals. Very early in its history, what were to be two of New York's most famous streets made their appearance: Broadway, which connected the town with farms further north; and Wall Street, named for the wall (actually, a wooden palisade) that was erected in 1633 to aid in the defense of the city from a threatened British attack. When the British did invade, they came by sea, and took over the Dutch possession in 1664. Under English rule New York began to grow beyond Wall Street, but this random expansion took place without any plan. By the end of the colonial period, the physical city had little left of its Dutch heritage. Its cobblestone-paved streets, lined with trees, and with houses built close together, presented a pleasing appearance. Its buildings were solid and handsome, but hardly any were outstanding.

The cities examined so far showed little evidence of rational planning; Philadelphia, on the other hand, was noted for the excellence of its plan. William Penn, the proprietor of the Pennsylvania colony, may be considered an early proponent of urban and regional planning. In July 1681 he told his commissioners who were to go to the colony with the first group of settlers that they were to establish a city as soon as possible. He provided them with fairly specific details about what that city was to be like, such as having a regular street pattern and uniform spacing of buildings. (*See Document No. 2.*) By the following summer, Captain Thomas Holme, Penn's surveyor general was laying out the city. The relatively flat land that Philadelphia occupied between the Schuylkill and Delaware rivers was arranged in a "gridiron" pattern, with straight streets intersecting each other at right angles. The grid was broken in several places by open squares, which were to be for the benefit of all the city's inhabitants. Although not a new concept, this was its first large-scale application in America. The naming of the streets was unusual for its time; those running north and south were numbered, while the intersecting streets were named for fruits and trees. One result of this was that Philadelphia was relatively easy to navigate. Another feature was that the city was to be separated from the countryside to the north by a green belt, known as "liberty lands." Unfortunately, as the city grew, some of the best features of the plan were violated. Philadelphia's plan was very influential in America. As will be discussed later, many new towns established in the American West borrowed Philadelphia's plan, although often without consideration of topography. Capitalizing on its excellent plan, Philadelphia, by the middle of the eighteenth century, was the most attractive and solid-looking city in Britain's American colonies.

Charles Town also was a planned city. Its plan consisted of an eight-block, irregular grid, surrounded by fortifications, but by 1717 the growth of the town resulted in a new plan. A gridiron design was adopted, with an open square at the intersection of the two principal streets. Unfortunately, little effort was made to preserve the square, and it was soon encroached upon. Still, Charles Town was considered a very attractive place. It had an appearance reminiscent of the West Indies. Among the most attractive elements were the homes of its wealthier residents, which often were faced with stucco colored in pastel shades, and graced by wrought-iron balconies. The most desirable place to have one of these homes would be along the waterfront, to take advantage of cool ocean breezes. A major fire in 1740 necessitated the rebuilding of much of the town. The new private homes were built in the same style as those they replaced, except that they were larger and more attractive. This also was when some handsome public buildings were erected, such as the State House and St. Michael's Church.

The Economic Base. As was noted previously, the five colonial cities owed their existence primarily to trade and commerce. Into them came goods from the mother country to be distributed throughout the colonies. In exchange, the products of the back country moved to these cities to be shipped to England and other markets. As trade grew, the urban merchants prospered, the standard of living increased, and the cities expanded in size and population. To meet the demands of the growth in population and wealth, merchants continually sought new areas of trade. There also was some development of industry in the cities, but these essentially were manufacturing operations that were related to trade, such as shipbuilding or preparation of materials for export.

For Boston, fish, especially cod, was at the center of the city's commerce. Caught principally off the banks of Newfoundland, the cod was salted, and then shipped to the Catholic countries of Europe and to the West Indies. In return, ships arrived in Boston Harbor with European luxury goods, molasses, rum, and Madeira and port wines. Boston also exported lumber and naval stores. As the principal importer of European goods to America, Boston had a thriving coastal trade with the other colonies until about 1730, when Philadelphia and New York made inroads into this trade. In addition to commerce, shipbuilding also added significantly to Boston's prosperity. As the city's merchant class increased in numbers and wealth, they gained status and influence in Boston society.

By the eighteenth century the merchants of Newport were important in the trade with the West Indies. Rum, molasses, and sugar were their specialties, and they were so successful that they took over much of this trade from Boston. Still, Newport had to rely on Boston for European manufactured goods. The slave trade was a major area of commerce for Newport, and her sea captains were the principal importers of slaves to

North America. Shipbuilding was an important activity, and in the 1740s Newport stole much of that business from Boston too.

Originally founded as a fur-trading center, New York's merchants gradually came to trade in a variety of products and with any ports where a profit could be made. The principal articles of export were bread, flour, and grain, and in the shipping of these products she was second only to Philadelphia. Trade with Great Britain increased constantly, and it achieved particular importance between 1750 and 1775. But trade with the Caribbean was also basic to the city's economy. The food products exported from New York were not well received in England, but they found good markets in the West Indies; and from those islands the New York merchants obtained products that could then be traded with England. Additionally, they had an extensive coastwise trade in food products and manufactured items, the largest volume of which was with the New England colonies. New Yorkers did especially well during the wars with France, when many of them were engaged in privateering, while others carried on a lucrative trade with the enemy. Since New York was the headquarters for the British forces in America during those years, supplying the British army was a particularly active business. These prosperous merchants were New York's aristocracy, and they provided the principal social, political, and intellectual leadership of the city. They became so successful that they had more capital available than their businesses could absorb, and so they began to turn to other sources of investment, such as loans, local government securities, real estate, marine insurance, and manufacturing. That manufacturing had to do with the repairing and outfitting of ships, rather than the building of them, and with the processing of raw materials for market.

The commercial prosperity of Philadelphia derived from an energetic merchant class and a productive hinterland, into which a series of roads were built to bring its resources to Philadelphia. And with the rapid growth in the population of western Pennsylvania, a market was created for the goods imported through Philadelphia. That city's commercial empire soon included portions of Delaware, Maryland, and western New Jersey. Wheat, flour, and livestock were shipped from Philadelphia especially to the West Indies and southern Europe, but Philadelphia's trade with Great Britain was less than that of Boston, New York, and Charles Town. Nonetheless, before the middle of the eighteenth century, Philadelphia's total volume of trade exceeded that of the other colonial cities. Like the other cities, its industrial activity, mainly ship-building and food processing, had to do with its commerce.

Lying much farther to the south, Charles Town's exports were of a much different nature. The principal products shipped from that city were deerskins, rice, and later indigo. Most of these goods were carried directly to England or southern Europe by Charles Town merchants, whose return cargoes were likely to be English manufactured goods, for which there was a local demand. These merchants also conducted a trade with the West Indies, from which they obtained slaves for work on the Carolina plantations. Slaves also were supplied by Newport traders, who brought them to Charles Town directly from Africa.

The People of the Cities. The colonial port towns not only acted as the reception centers for European and West Indian goods, into them also came people from Europe and Africa. Most of these people, especially during the seventeenth century, were from England, but many came from other countries. Important elements in the colonies came from Ireland, Scotland, Wales, Germany, France, and Africa. Although most of these people ultimately became engaged in agricultural pursuits and helped push the frontier westward, many remained in the port cities. Indeed, the increasingly cosmopolitan atmosphere of most of these cities became a major factor in distinguishing them from the countryside.

One of the earliest non-English groups to have a profound impact on the composition of the colonial cities were the Africans, who were brought to America as slaves. They were most numerous in Charles Town, where, by the eighteenth century, they accounted for approximately half the population. There were a smaller, but significant, element of the population of New York, where they comprised a quarter of the residents by 1720. In the same year, approximately a sixth of Boston's population was African. In Philadelphia and Newport their numbers were much smaller.

The ingredients of the populations of each of the colonial ports were quite different. Boston contained very few non-English residents during its early years, although that changed slightly as some Scotch-Irish settled there after 1720. Still, only a very small percentage of the non-English migration to America ended up in Boston. In fact, Boston actually attempted to restrict non-English immigration. Still, Newport, except for some Africans imported as servants, was even more homogeneous; only a very few Scotch-Irish and Germans settled there. New York, on the other hand, began as a very cosmopolitan place and it continued that way throughout the colonial period. Under the Dutch, it was home to people of various nationalities. And under the English the population continued to be mixed, as Scotch-Irish, Germans, Africans, and a variety of other peoples were added to the mix. Philadelphia, too, had a varied composition. Although originally settled by English Quakers, by the 1720s Philadelphia contained a large representation of non-English residents. Largely as a result of William Penn's very active advertising of his colony, Philadelphia became the main port of entry for Scotch-Irish and German migrants to the colonies, and while the majority settled in the interior, a considerable number remained in Philadelphia. While the English-speaking Scotch-Irish quickly blended in with the rest of the population, the Germans tended to group together and retain their own language and culture. These are the people who later came to be called the "Pennsylvania Dutch," who, of course, were not Dutch. The name was a corruption of "Deutsch," the German word for "German." Earlier, migrants from Wales had settled in Philadelphia and the surrounding area, and the names of many communities in the region reflect their Welch origins. A varied population also was to be found in Charles Town. The large African element already has been noted, but the city contained a variety of other peoples as well. The city originally had been settled primarily by English migrants from Barbados, who moved there with their African slaves. Even before the eighteenth century some French Huguenots took up residence in Charles Town, and in the 1720s some Scotch-Irish and Swiss were added to the population.

These various peoples settled in the young cities of America for many reasons, but most were driven by a hope for economic betterment. For some, there were religious and political reasons for migration, and for others, particularly the Africans, the movement was not a result of choice. The society that emerged in these cities was somewhat more fluid than that of Europe, but social structure reflected considerable inequality nonetheless. By and large, government and social life was dominated by men of wealth and status. There were a considerable number of poor people in each town almost from the outset, and the poor were becoming more numerous. Still, while it was very difficult to move upward in society, it was possible, and there were some who managed to improve their status.

The Development of Urban Services. The gathering together of people into an urban environment gives rise to a variety of needs and problems. Today, we expect that a city will attend to these by providing for the health, safety, and general welfare of its inhabitants. This is accomplished, for example, by maintaining fire, police, and sanitation departments, and by seeing to it that city streets are maintained and well-lighted, and that there is an adequate supply of pure water. The colonial cities were faced with these needs and problems, and they tried to address them in a variety of ways.

Fire was an ever-present and serious menace. Fire prevention and fire fighting could be left up to an individual only insofar as his own dwelling or shop was concerned; but one could not vouch for one's neighbor. In an urban environment buildings are close together, and especially during the colonial period, they were constructed of combustible materials. The outbreak of a fire in one building was thus a danger to the entire town. Clearly, preventing and fighting fires became a community problem. To prevent the outbreak of fires the towns passed various ordinances regulating the types of building materials that could be used, requiring that chimneys be cleaned regularly, prohibiting bonfires and fireworks, and other similar legislation. Individual citizens also often were required to keep fire-fighting equipment, and the towns themselves maintained equipment for combating fire. Usually, people volunteered to help extinguish fires in the part of the town in which they lived, but frequently local ordinances required this activity. There were some attempts to establish regular fire departments in the eighteenth century, but for the most part fire fighting was not a professional function.

Preserving the public peace was another urban problem that required communal, rather than individual, action, and that was recognized from the outset. Since there were no organized, uniformed police in England or Holland, it should not be a surprise that there were none in the American colonies. To protect their citizens at night, most towns provided for some sort of night watch, usually comprised of residents who took turns patrolling the streets. For daytime protection, the towns employed constables, who were usually elected to one-year terms of office. The prestige of that job was low, and it often was difficult to find men willing to serve. Many citizens objected to the establishment of regular police forces, fearing that they might be used as instruments of repression.

Town officials realized that well-lighted streets might help prevent crimes. In the early years they tried to accomplish this by requiring homeowners to place candles in their front windows or keep lanterns outside, but gradually the town governments began to provide lamps in the streets. By the time of the Revolution, all the towns except Newport were providing tax-supported street lighting. These street lamps apparently were very attractive to vandals, and so the towns passed laws providing for substantial fines for anyone found guilty of breaking them.

The condition of streets was very important to these communities because of their function in the movement of goods; and so by the beginning of the eighteenth century most of the colonial towns were making an effort to pave and repair their streets. Indeed, a considerable portion of each town's budget often was expended for street surfacing and repair. The only city to have unpaved streets throughout this period was Charles Town. Newport, on the other hand, was quite innovative in finding funds for street paving. At first a portion of the duty collected on slaves imported into Newport financed street surfacing, but later the money was raised through a lottery. If most of these towns expended considerable sums of money on street surfacing and repair, it was rare that much effort went into street sanitation. In the early years garbage would lie in the streets until consumed by animals or washed away by rain; but by the middle of the eighteenth century some of the town governments were hiring men to clean the streets from time to time, although provision for regular street cleaning was unusual.

An adequate supply of water is essential to the existence of a city, and the colonial town governments tried to see that it was provided. However, the need of water for drinking was not a primary concern, for water was not the most popular beverage in colonial American. More important was that water be available to fight fires. Water generally was obtained from wells, most of which were private. But private wells might present a problem in case of fire, so public wells were dug after a while. Not only did these public wells provide a source of water for fire fighting, they also served poorer residents who could not afford to have their own wells. Water for drinking purposes usually would be obtained from springs outside of town, and it sometimes was sold by street vendors.

If these attempts at providing urban services seem primitive by modern standards, they probably were adequate for the small cities of the colonial era, and they certainly were no worse than what existed in the cities of England. Governments provided only those services that were deemed absolutely necessary and that could not be supplied through private initiative. For the most part, this attitude has prevailed throughout the history of urban America.

The Manifestations of Culture. In Colonial America most manifestations of culture were to be found in the cities. There were some erudite individuals living on plantations, but this did not provide for the makings of a significant cultural atmosphere. Just as European goods and peoples came into the cities and spread out from them, so too did European ideas and culture. City life permitted frequent contact with others and the interchange of ideas. And the increasing urban populations and growing prosperity made feasible the establishment of cultural agencies such as schools, libraries, printing and publishing establishments, bookstores, and theaters. The existence of these agencies fostered creative energies in art, science, and literature.

Until the middle of the eighteenth century, Boston was the cultural center of the colonies, with a tradition for learning that dated back to its earliest years. Bostonians both read and wrote. Most wealthy citizens had good personal libraries, and the city contained many bookshops. There was a considerable literary output from its citizens, and the city became an important publishing center. It also was the premier art center in American until mid-eighteenth century, counting among its citizens John Singleton Copley, without doubt the finest colonial American painter. But by the mid-1700s, Boston was supplanted by Philadelphia as America's cultural leader. Not only did several Philadelphia citizens have substantial private libraries, but several libraries were established that were open to some elements of the public. In the number of bookshops and as a publishing center Philadelphia also pulled ahead of Boston. There was considerable activity in writing in Philadelphia, the best of which was political writing. And some excellent painters resided there, most notable among them were Benjamin West and Charles Willson Peale. Certainly, too, Philadelphia was the leading center for scientific inquiry in the colonies. Among its citizens were such outstanding scientists as Benjamin Franklin, John Bartram, Benjamin Rush, and David Rittenhouse.

While there were many learned individuals among the residents of New York, the production of literature and art did not compare with

Boston or Philadelphia. Nonetheless, there was a cultural atmosphere in the city, which contained libraries and bookstores, and whose citizens showed considerable interest in music and theater. New Yorkers seemed to enjoy those aspects of culture that brought them into social contact with other people. In essence, the culture of New York was a gregarious one, rather than a productive one. A similar situation existed in Charles Town, where culture was confined largely to wealthy planters and merchants. These people were patrons of the arts, rather than producers of them. Visiting painters, for example, found many customers in Charles Town, and musical and theatrical performances were very popular in that city.

Although the extent and quality of education varied from town to town, it was easier to obtain an education in urban than in rural areas. While the rich were more likely to be educated than the poor everywhere, this was more true in the rural portions of the colonies. Wealthy planters frequently hired private tutors for their sons, and they often sent them to England to be educated, but these were not options for poor farmers. In the cities, however, education was more widely available, with each of the five towns providing some facilities for public education by the eighteenth century. And prior to 1760, three of the five towns contained institutions of higher learning.

The Political Impact of Urbanization. As the colonial cities grew in population, commerce, and wealth, their influence became increasingly important. This growing influence was nowhere more apparent than in the events leading up to the most significant political event of the era, the American Revolution. One leading historian has maintained that the cities served to prepare the social and intellectual groundwork for independence. American nationality, he claimed, developed in the cities—not in the rural areas, where provincial attachment held out longer. Unity arose from the cities and their common interests. "Constant communication, arising out of the needs of commerce, served to forge these communities into an integrated urban society—the only segment of colonial population so fused."[1] As noted, European ideas, such as those of John Locke and other political philosophers, entered America through the cities and were disseminated from them. In this

[1] Carl Bridenbaugh, *Cities in Revolt: Urban Life in America, 1743–1776* (New York: Alfred A. Knopf, 1968), 418.

regard, the libraries, publishing houses, bookshops, and newspapers of the cities were very important. But it would take more than ideas to bring about a revolution; there were some very practical considerations as well. Urban merchants felt the impact of British trade regulations, and this group provided significant leadership for opposition to British policies. Later, leadership came from urban lawyers and politicians.

The role of Boston was especially important. On the eve of the Revolution, Boston's position no longer was what it had been earlier in the colonial period. In both commerce and population Boston had fallen behind Philadelphia and New York, and Boston was no longer the leading cultural center in the colonies. Because of her declining position, a distinguished historian has noted, Boston may have been "resolved at any cost to stay the throttling hand of Parliament."[2] With the levying of the Coercive Acts against Boston in 1774, the movement toward revolution began to come to a head, and, as another historian has noted, if the background to the Revolution is examined in this light, then "the American Revolution began on the cobblestones of Boston rather than on the rolling greens of Lexington."[3]

The influence of the cities also may be seen in what has often been perceived as a conflict between East and West that was noticeable in the years prior to independence and also during the period of the Confederation. In actuality, this may have been an urban-rural conflict. Certainly, to some degree, urban interests were of importance in the framing of the Constitution. How great a role the urban businessmen played in this has been disputed, but that they did play a major role is clear, and that is of great significance since these urban businessmen represented only a very small segment of the population. Out of this urban-rural conflict so prevalent in the formative years of the nation came the subsequent development of political parties.

[2] Arthur M. Schlesinger, *Paths to the Present* (New York: Macmillan, 1949), 213.
[3] Richard C. Wade, "The City in History—Some American Perspectives," in *American Life and Form*, ed. Werner Z. Hirsch (New York: Holt, Rinehart and Winston, 1965), 63.

CHAPTER 2

THE CITIES OF THE NEW NATION: 1790–1820

The years from 1790–1820 do not represent a period of tremendous urban growth. The first United States census in 1790 found that only 5.1 percent of Americans could be classed as urban dwellers. By 1820 that number had increased, but the urban population was still a small minority of the total population, amounting to 7.2 percent. Nevertheless, even though fewer than one in ten Americans lived in cities, the urban sector played a very important role in many facets of American life.

The Eastern Cities. In 1790 Philadelphia was the largest city in the United States, with a population of 42,560. New York's 33,131 people put it in second place, followed by Boston, Charleston (formerly Charles Town), and Baltimore, each of which contained fewer than twenty thousand residents. If total urban growth in America was not dramatic during these years, several of the eastern cities experienced significant population increases. This period also saw a shift in the rank order of these cities. By 1820, New York was the largest city in the nation, a position which it never relinquished. Its population in that year was 123,706. Although Philadelphia's population increased substantially to 112,772, that city was now in second place. Boston (43,298) lost its third place position to Baltimore (62,738), and the fifth largest city was a newcomer, New Orleans (27,200), which became part of the United States with the 1803 Louisiana Purchase.

Although Boston had slipped to fourth place in population, it was growing nonetheless, and it remained a busy and important city. It was also an attractive city, in no small way due to the work of the architect Charles Bulfinch. His most prominent work was the design of the Massachusetts State House, which was completed in 1798. This red brick building with white marble trim was surmounted by a dome, which was the first in Boston. The building set a precedent for capitol architecture in America. Most new state capitols were to be domed, and so, too, was the national capitol. The Boston State House led to the residential development of Beacon Hill, on which it stood, and many of those homes were designed by Bulfinch. Bulfinch also designed several residential streets and churches, rebuilt and enlarged Faneuil Hall, and was the architect of a number of commercial structures. It is no wonder that the city of this era has been dubbed "Bulfinch's Boston."

Boston's very large harbor continued to foster a thriving commerce, but shipbuilding, manufacturing, cod fishing, and whaling also added substantially to the city's economy. Economic growth led to physical growth, and because of Boston being connected to the rest of Massachusetts by only a narrow neck of land, this meant building several bridges over the Charles River. Goods and people moving any distance from Boston went by water, but some roads were built linking Boston with other communities. Overland travel, though, was very slow. In the first decade of the nineteenth century a stagecoach trip from Boston to New York took six days.

There might be many reasons for making a trip to New York, for these were the years during which that city began its great growth. By 1810 New York had moved ahead of Philadelphia to become the largest city in the United States, and it increased its lead by 1820. This, of course, was a source of great dismay to Philadelphians, and an intense rivalry between these two cities began during this period and persisted for many years. Geographic location was very important to New York's commercial rise: It had an excellent harbor and it was well located for coastwise trade; Boston was the only major city closer to Europe. There were other major factors, too, that contributed to New York's dominance during this period and beyond, and these will be discussed later. But even by 1815, New York's foreign commerce already was twice that of either Boston or Philadelphia. This prosperity, however, was not evident from the city's appearance. New York was not a very imposing place during this period. The principal street was Broadway, which was built up for about two miles. At the tip of Broadway, near the Battery, were the homes of the city's leading merchants. Farther up were well-stocked shops of all types, and at what at that time was the far end of Broadway, stood New York's City Hall, which was completed in 1812, and which was undoubtedly the handsomest building in the city. Broadway, which had poplar trees planted on either side, may have been a reasonably attractive street, but for the most part the streets of New York were filthy. In addition to horses, a variety of animals, both alive and dead, were commonly seen in the city's streets.

New York continued to be the cosmopolitan city it had been since its founding. A new element was added to the population when, after the

French revolution, a number of French emigres settled in the city. Although New York is not usually thought of as a city where slavery prevailed, the 1790 census revealed that approximately one-ninth of the city's population were Africans, two-thirds of whom were held as slaves. The city's mixed population continued to prefer cultural activities that brought them into contact with others, so that theater and music remained popular. By 1800 New York had two playhouses, one of which, the Park Theater, built in 1798, was reputed to have been able to accommodate an audience of two thousand.

Although surpassed by New York as the nation's largest city, Philadelphia enjoyed considerable growth in population and prosperity. It still retained its financial leadership, and it engaged in a substantial foreign commerce. Philadelphia also was well located for trade with the American West, but that commerce was not yet well developed. A major feature of the city that was important to its commercial prosperity, was a large arcaded market that extended for nearly a mile and a half along the center of the main street. That street, originally named High Street, had its name changed to Market Street in 1790 in recognition of that structure. Interestingly, many American towns have imitated Philadelphia and named their principal streets Market Street, even though those streets did not contain public markets.

Cobblestone streets, red brick sidewalks, and three-story houses of red brick and white marble trim, were common in Philadelphia, and provided the city with both texture and color. Those streets were kept reasonably clean, since Philadelphia was the first city to take on regular street cleaning as a municipal function. Street sanitation was made easier as a result of Philadelphia also becoming the first city to build a municipal waterworks. The decision to undertake that project was made in 1797 in reaction to the 1793 yellow fever epidemic that took the lives of thousands of Philadelphians, in the hope that a better water supply would help avert such a catastrophe in the future. The system was designed by the noted architect, Benjamin Latrobe, and it was completed in 1801. Steam-operated pumps drew the water from the Schuylkill River, and it was distributed to users through bored logs. This system not only was important to the residents of the city, it also became a very popular tourist attraction. Visitors were fascinated by the machinery as well as the handsome classical architecture of the structures that housed it.

The fastest growing Atlantic port was Baltimore; a city of only 6,000 inhabitants at the beginning of the Revolution, it contained nearly

63,000 residents by 1820. It had an excellent location on the Patapsco River, with an outlet to the sea through Chesapeake Bay. Baltimore also was well placed to obtain products from the west, and soon came to dominate the grain and tobacco trade of Virginia, Maryland, and central Pennsylvania. As important as location was, it was not the only reason for the city's success. The energetic merchants of Baltimore worked hard to improve the city's commercial position by improving the harbor, erecting wharves and warehouses, expanding shipbuilding, and building a system of turnpikes to tap the interior. Some manufacturing also was developed, especially flour milling and whiskey distilling, which added to the value of the grain brought into the city.

It will be remembered that during the Colonial Period Charleston had been a major port, but by 1820 it was only of secondary importance in foreign trade. There were several reasons for this. Cotton growing became the major agricultural activity of the South, and cotton culture was moving westward. Savannah was better located to receive and ship cotton, and that city offered stiff competition to Charleston. Then, too, as will be discussed later, New York merchants gradually took over Charleston's cotton trade. Still, if Charleston's population and trade did not increase very much, the city still was the center for the Carolina planter, and it was considered a very attractive place. It was run by a planter oligarchy, and for them it was a very pleasant place where they could enjoy balls, concerts, dinner parties, and horse races.

The Choice of a Capital City. One of the most significant decisions that needed to be made for the newly-formed United States of America was where to place the national capital. During the Revolution, Philadelphia mainly served that function, but Baltimore, Lancaster, and York hosted the Continental Congress for brief periods. Once the war was concluded, the new nation's government moved to Princeton, Annapolis, Trenton, and New York. Being designated the capital not only would bring prestige to a community, but even the minimal activities of the government of that time would bring some economic advantage. It is no wonder, then, that several communities petitioned Congress for the honor. Kingston (N.Y.), Annapolis, Williamsburg, Newport, Wilmington, Reading, New York, and Philadelphia were among the hopefuls. So when the new Congress formed by the Constitution met in 1789, there was considerable debate over the location of the capital. Unable to resolve the question, debate continued the next year, when it was decided to resolve the problem by establishing a federal district on the Potomac River. That decision came about primarily as a result of a deal arranged by two of the nation's most powerful political leaders, Thomas Jefferson and Alexander Hamilton. Hamilton would have preferred a northern location, but he was more interested in having the federal government assume the debts contracted by the states during the Revolution, while Jefferson's views were the opposite. The compromise was that Jefferson would support the state debt assumption and, in return, Hamilton would support a southern location for the capital.

The actual site for the new city was chosen by George Washington, who appointed a noted surveyor, Andrew Ellicott, to establish the boundaries of the district. Major Pierre Charles L'Enfant was to prepare the plan for the city. His plan called for a grid design, intersected by wide diagonal avenues that would link the principal sites. The reasons for this were not only aesthetic; L'Enfant hoped these broad avenues would help spur settlement over the whole area of the city by appearing to reduce distances. He envisioned these avenues as being lined with trees, with the principal thoroughfare (Pennsylvania Avenue) connecting the president's house with the Capitol. (*See Document No. 3.*) Needing to raise money for building construction, the government decided to have a public sale of lots in the new city in the fall of 1791. L'Enfant was asked to have copies of his plan printed for distribution, and to have it displayed at the auction. L'Enfant refused to do either, believing that if prospective purchasers knew where lots were located in relation to public buildings the widespread settlement of the district would be retarded. Partly for his intransigence, L'Enfant was dismissed, and Ellicott produced the map using L'Enfant's drawings.

The map was impressive, but the reality was not. In the early years, Washington grew very slowly. A visitor of this period would have some difficulty in determining where many of the streets were located. With cattle grazing on the Mall and vegetable gardens in the squares, Washington certainly did not present an urban prospect. The nation's capital came to be mocked as "The City of Magnificent Intentions" or "The City of Magnificent Distances."

The Westward Movement of Cities. Another important aspect of the history of the American city during this period was the movement of urbanization into the Ohio Valley. By 1820 the largest cities in that region were Cincinnati (9,642), Pittsburgh (7,248), Lexington (5,279), St. Louis (4,598), and Louisville (4,012). These were small places, but they clearly were urban. It is interesting to note that the founding of these cities usually came before the establishment of farms. While many settlers of the American West sought farmland, many others journeyed westward seeking to gain wealth through the founding of towns. After all, an investment in urban land potentially would yield faster and greater returns than an investment in agricultural land, and there were substantial business opportunities to be found in newly established cities.

St. Louis was the oldest of these cities. It was established in 1763 by a New Orleans firm to act as a fur-trading post. In part because it originally was not conceived as a potentially large settlement, it had a carelessly conceived plan borrowed from New Orleans. At first the town grew very slowly, with its main growth coming after the Louisiana Purchase. Pittsburgh was nearly as old, receiving its first town plan in 1764. That city certainly had an excellent location at the point where the Monongahela and Allegheny rivers meet to form the Ohio River. Unfortunately, Pittsburgh's 1784 plan, which established the configuration of the city, was a disaster, laying out a gridiron pattern on land that was hilly and triangular in shape. Starting slowly, Pittsburgh's population began to grow in the 1790s. Louisville owed its origin to the Revolution, when George Rogers Clark established it in 1778 to use it as a base for military operations against the British. By 1780 a rectangular town plan began to be laid out. That plan originally called for a fair amount of publicly held land, but the town's debts resulted in that land being sold. This was most unfortunate, especially as the town grew, since it left no land for parks or public buildings. (*See Document No. 4.*) Although advantageously located at the Falls of the Ohio, Louisville grew very slowly before 1800. Less well sited for future growth was Lexington, the only one of these towns not located near a navigable waterway. First settled in 1779, Lexington adopted a gridiron plan in 1781. Although it was the largest town in the region by 1800, its population leadership was to be short-lived. More promising for the future was the Ohio River town of Cincinnati. First inhabited at the end of 1788, Cincinnati was named for a Revolutionary War veterans' society in the early 1790s. The town was laid out in a regular grid pattern closely based on that of Philadelphia. Although its early years were marked by floods and trouble with Indians, Cincinnati grew rapidly.

It is noteworthy that the planners of each of these towns laid out streets using a rectangular grid pattern, and all of them, with the exception of St. Louis, borrowed from the plan of Philadelphia. Certainly a grid plan had the advantage of making surveying easier and faster. Then, too, Philadelphia was the largest and most important city in England's American colonies and the early United States, so it is not surprising that it would serve as a model for the founders of these communities. But perhaps there was a deeper significance for the adoption of this plan. As one historian has pointed out: "It represented the difference between town organization and country life. . . . Early planners connected regularity in design with cities, and refused to make any deviation, even when the configuration of the terrain suggested it."[4] The results of this rigid commitment to a grid pattern were not always very good, especially from an aesthetic standpoint. Philadelphia's plan was placed on land that was fairly flat and bounded by two rivers running roughly parallel at that point. In Pittsburgh, for example, the grid was imposed on a hilly, triangular-shaped parcel of land, requiring two grids placed at an angle to each other. Cincinnati, too, was a city of hills, and the Ohio River curved along its shoreline. Furthermore, the planners often ignored some of the best features of the Philadelphia plan, in particular the provision for open squares.

To a great extent, the appearance of these cities was a result of their commercial orientation. They were all founded as centers of commerce, and their early growth came with the expansion of commercial activity into this newly settled western region. (*See Document No. 5.*)

Although Pittsburgh's economy primarily benefited from commerce during its early years, there were some signs of the city's future industrial development. Pittsburgh was located on the best route to the new western areas, but because of the difficulty of crossing the Appalachians, few manufactured items were transported by western migrants. This presented a great opportunity for local merchants, and it stimulated the development of manufacturing in the city. During these years we find the beginnings of what were to be two of Pittsburgh's leading industries, the manufacture of iron and glass.

Connected by roads to the Ohio River and to Virginia and the Carolinas, Lexington served the farmers of Kentucky and Tennessee as a cen-

[4] Richard C. Wade, *The Urban Frontier: The Rise of Western Cities, 1790–1830* (Cambridge, MA: Harvard University Press, 1959), 28.

tral distributing market. While most of Lexington's merchants invested their profits in land, some saw manufacturing as a potentially lucrative source of income. The main industrial pursuit was the processing of hemp, but a variety of other manufacturing also developed. It should be noted that slave labor was fairly extensively used in Lexington's factories. While Lexington prospered for a while, not being located near a navigable waterway was to prove a major handicap, especially with the appearance of the steamboat.

Unlike the citizens of Pittsburgh and Lexington, those of Cincinnati were devoting very little attention to industrial development. The merchants of Cincinnati profited from purchases made by western migrants, and these merchants acquired the products from Philadelphia, Baltimore, and New Orleans. The Ohio River provided them with a highway for the distribution of these goods in Kentucky, Indiana, and Ohio. Except for the disruption of trade during and immediately after the War of 1812, there was little incentive to develop much manufacturing, and the industrial activity that took place during those years, received a major setback by the postwar depression.

St. Louis, located farther west than the other towns in the region, developed slowly because problems with the local Indians deterred settlers. The presence of troops during the War of 1812 brought a measure of security, and along with that a population increase. The most important economic activity in St. Louis was the fur trade, and there also was some development of the lead industry. The principal sources of goods for local merchants were Philadelphia and Baltimore, with some coming upriver from New Orleans.

Louisville, located near the Falls of the Ohio, prospered from the transshipment of goods around that obstacle to navigation. (*See Document No. 4.*) The unloading and loading of boats and the movement of merchandise certainly added to the city's economy, but so, too, did the money spent in town by travelers and traders. This commercial activity attracted population.

As these western cities grew in population, they had to contend with a variety of problems. One of the most pressing was the condition of the streets. As commercial centers, street paving was vital for the movement of goods, and so street improvement took up a considerable portion of the budgets of these towns, some of which actually established departments to oversee the work. Despite this expenditure and effort, streets were mostly not well paved. Fire protection was another serious concern, since fires in these wood-built cities occurred frequently. Building materials were regulated by local ordinances, which also were aimed at eliminating fire hazards. At first, all town residents were responsible for fighting fires, but gradually volunteer fire companies took over the task. Some sort of policing was necessary from the outset, but it remained rather unorganized except in those towns that had significant slave populations. Providing for an adequate supply of water was not a problem in the early years, since each of the towns, with the exception of Lexington, was located near a river, and Lexington was able to draw water from a spring. Although public wells were provided, there were no public water systems.

While demonstrating an adventurous spirit in moving out to what were new frontiers, the founders and early leaders of these cities were not very original in their approaches to urban life. The models for almost everything they did were the eastern cities. New York and Boston often provided those models, but Philadelphia was by far the leading example. It already has been noted that most of them borrowed their original plans from Philadelphia, and they also looked to Philadelphia in their approach to dealing with urban problems. Cincinnati's imitation of Philadelphia was so apparent that visitors frequently commented on how similar the two cities were, at least in appearance. The western cities also reproduced the stratified society that their inhabitants had known in eastern cities. Thus, imitation, rather than innovation, characterized these new cities of the Ohio Valley region.

CHAPTER 3

AN ERA OF RAPID URBAN GROWTH: 1820–1860

Characteristics of Urban Growth. The years 1820–1860 constitute an extremely important period in the development of American cities. During this period cities grew at the most rapid rate in the history of the United States. Between 1820 and 1860 the total population of the United States grew by 226 percent, but the urban population increased by 797 percent. Each decennial census revealed that the nation's population had grown by approximately one third, while the 1820s and '30s each accounted for a nearly two-thirds increase in the urban population. The high point came in the 1840s; during that decade the urban population increased by just over 92 percent, which was the most significant increase in the nation's history. Urban growth declined slightly in percentage during the 1850s, although not in numbers; but still managed to increase by more than 75 percent. The most rapid growth occurred in the larger cities. Between 1820 and 1860 all cities increased nine times in population, while cities of more than 50,000 inhabitants in 1820 increased twelve time in population. By 1860, nine cities contained 100,000 or more residents; an additional twenty-five cities had populations of 25,000 or more; and there were four hundred cities of lesser populations. In 1820 there had been only sixty-two urban places. The growth of some specific cities had been dramatic. The largest cities were still in the east, led by New York, which had grown from123,706 in 1820, to 813,669 in 1860. Philadelphia was in second place (112,772 to 565,529), followed by Brooklyn (11,187 to 279,122), Baltimore (62,738 to 212,418), and Boston (43,298 to 177,840). Some cities of the Ohio and Mississippi River regions grew at an astonishing rate during these years; the largest of these were New Orleans (27,176 to 168,675), Cincinnati (9,642 to 161,044), and St. Louis (4,598 to 160,773). But it was a city of the Great Lakes region, Chicago, that witnessed the most exciting growth of all. In 1830, there were only fifty people living in that settlement, but by 1860 the population of Chicago was 112,172, ranking it as the ninth largest city in the United States!

The creation of new cities during this period was to a large degree a result of the development of the West. As we have seen, the westward movement spawned towns as well as farms. Indeed, one of the things that pulled people westward was the promotional schemes of town-site speculators. Cities sprang up in the West to serve as centers of commerce (river ports, lake ports) and as administrative centers. The northern portion was becoming more urbanized than the southern portion. The small farms of the northern region were more dependent on local trade centers than were the plantations of the southern region. There also was more fluid capital in the North. The cities that developed relied upon good transportation facilities for their continued growth.

As was noted earlier, the Ohio River was the first area of mid-western urban growth, with its principal centers being Pittsburgh, Cincinnati, and Louisville. Next came the junction of the Mississippi and Ohio Rivers. Here, Cairo was founded, but it never developed into a major city; but St. Louis, at the junction of the Mississippi and Missouri, did develop into a great city. Some of the western cities grew larger than others because they became central distribution points for the other cities. As land was taken up settlers moved out from the Ohio area. During the 1840s and '50s they moved into the Great Lakes area. At this time the lake cities (Buffalo, Cleveland, Chicago) began to come into focus. Chicago became the greatest of these cities, since it had the position as a major lake port and as a railroad hub. Still other new towns developed in the United States as a result of manufacturing or mining, or they emerged as administrative centers.

People were pulled to these cities by the greater economic advantages that existed in them. The basic foundations of the urban economy in the pre-Civil War period were trade and commerce. The acceleration of trade and commerce that occurred between 1820 and 1860 throughout the nation was a major stimulant to urban growth. The great increase in trade resulted from the growth of the nation, both in population and area, but it also was partly a consequence of the increased commercial intercourse of the United States with the rest of the world. The capacity to capitalize on these commercial opportunities affected the comparative prosperity of individual cities.

The Growth of New York City. Certainly no city capitalized on commercial opportunities with greater success than New York. Before 1820 New York had moved ahead of the other Atlantic ports, and in the years that followed it extended its lead over them in both population and importance. This was partly due to the city's natural advantages; it had a good location, an excellent harbor, and a large and valuable hinterland. Still, the other Atlantic ports also were well located, Boston had an excellent harbor, and Philadelphia and Baltimore had rich and extensive hinterlands. But the citizens of New York were particularly innovative and energetic, and they initiated actions to promote their city's commercial leadership. The most significant of these were the establishment of an attractive auction system for disposing of imports, the establishment of regular transatlantic packet service, the development of what was known as the "cotton triangle," and the building of the Erie Canal.

Auction sales themselves were not an innovation; they had been used in America's ports for many years, but they had been used mainly to dispose of damaged or surplus goods. In New York auction sales were more widely used than elsewhere, and in 1817 the taxes on those sales in New York were reduced, and legislation was passed requiring that goods put up for sale must be sold to the highest bidder. These developments worked out very well for both seller and buyer. The buyer could hope to get the goods for a lower price, and the seller could afford to sell the goods for a lower price because a quick sale would mean savings on storage and insurance.

Before packet lines (two or more ships sailing definite routes on set schedules) began service in New York, shippers could not be sure when ships containing their goods would leave port or when they would return with imports. Frequently, too, they were not even certain of the route. At the beginning of January 1818, packet service was introduced out of New York by the Black Ball Line. Each month, at a specified day and hour, one of their ships would sail from New York and another from Liverpool. By 1822 the Black Ball Line had increased its sailings to twice a month from each port. During the next few years other New York packet line companies were formed, and by 1845 there were fifty-two transatlantic packets making three regular sailings from New York each week. This regular service soon attracted to the packets the cream of the transatlantic business—mail, cabin passengers, and the highest-paying freight. Packet service from other ports, which got underway later, was never as successful as that from New York.

The cotton triangle was a particularly significant development. Its three corners were a cotton port (Charleston, Savannah, Mobile, or New Orleans), a European port (usually Liverpool or Le Havre), and New York. Most ships sailed the three sides of the triangle, carrying cotton directly from the southern port to Europe, returning to New York with general freight or immigrants, and heading back to the southern port with freight or in ballast. New York was affected even more directly when only two sides of the triangle were used, in which the voyage from the southern port to Europe was eliminated. Both methods were profitable to New York merchants, though, and soon New York came to take over a large share of the South's commercial activity. By 1822 the cotton triangle trade was well established. While the inauguration of packet line service and the opening of the Erie Canal were both announced with substantial fanfare, the cotton triangle was developed gradually and quietly, for fear of alarming the southern ports. Since cotton was the principal export of the United States in the years before the Civil War, this trade was of major importance to New York; so much so, that when the South seceded from the Union in 1861, the New York City Common Council seriously considered a measure for New York to secede as well!

The completion of the Erie Canal from Albany to Buffalo in 1825 brought more materials for export into New York and also greatly increased the market for goods the city imported. (The building of the Erie Canal and its effects will be discussed later.) These developments brought about by the energy of New York's citizens, combined with the city's natural advantages, propelled the port to dominance in American foreign trade. For the period 1821–1860 New York accounted for 60 percent of the nation's total imports and 33 percent of its exports.

Tapping the Hinterland: Transportation and Urban Imperialism.

To ensure their continued commercial prosperity, each of the Atlantic Coast cities attempted to develop its hinterland during this period. This quest for expanding markets and sources of raw materials resulted in considerable rivalry among these cities.

New York's original hinterland consisted of the Hudson Valley and other upstate New York regions, and parts of Long Island, New Jersey, and Connecticut. To improve the city's trade connections with upstate New York, the establishment of an all-water route across the state that would link the Hudson River with Lake Erie had been proposed for many years, going back as early as the late-eighteenth century. Doing so, though, would involve the construction of a several-hundred-mile-long canal, at a time when there were fewer than a hundred miles of canal in the entire country. Moreover, the United States lacked engineers, since the military academy at West Point was the only school that trained engineers at all. Possibly because there were no engineers to point out that building such a canal would be an impossible task, the impossible became a reality. In 1817 work began on the Erie Canal. The project proceeded very rapidly, and it was completed between Albany and Buffalo in 1825. The canal was very important to the commercial development of New York City. Combined with the city's dominance in the cotton trade, it resulted in much of the country becoming New York's hinterland by the 1840s.

Not only was the Erie Canal of major significance for New York City, it also was very important to the urban development of western New York State. It brought substantial prosperity to Albany, located at the eastern terminus of the canal. Utica prospered as a major canal port, and Syracuse owed its origin to the Erie Canal. Rochester, located on the Genessee River, grew tremendously following completion of the canal. In 1812 Rochester had only fifteen inhabitants, and it had grown to only 331 by 1816. But the canal connection brought increased trade and population. By 1840 Rochester was the nation's leading flour-milling center, and it had a population of 20,000. Lockport, located at the point where a series of locks had to be constructed to bring the canal over the so-called Mountain Ridge, owed its origin to the Erie Canal. Buffalo, located where the canal met Lake Erie, became a boom town in these years. Although it is true that Buffalo was more of a lake port than a canal town, if it were not for the Erie Canal Buffalo would not have had so many lake boats docking there.

The great success enjoyed by the Erie Canal was not exactly welcomed by New York's rival Atlantic Coast cities. Before the canal was completed, Philadelphia and Baltimore, linked to the Ohio Valley by turnpikes, had a substantial advantage in the western trade. But that trade had consisted more of manufactured goods moving west, rather than agricultural products moving east, since it was easier and cheaper to ship those bulky cargoes down the Mississippi to New Orleans. The Erie Canal, however, provided an excellent two-way system, and it immediately began to take trade away from the turnpikes. Clearly, the other Atlantic ports would have to establish more efficient transportation links to the west if they were to stay competitive with New York. New York, though, had a geographical advantage with the Mohawk Valley, which was the only good route through the Appalachian barrier.

Still, the other ports took action to meet the competition. As the Erie

Canal was nearing completion in 1825, the Pennsylvania Canal Commissioners recommended construction of a canal from Philadelphia to
Pittsburgh, and an act authorizing it was passed the next year. In 1834,
what was known as the Mainline Canal was completed. It was not simply
a canal, but a hodgepodge of various means of transportation, consisting of a railroad from Philadelphia to the Susquehanna River, a canal to
the eastern end of the mountains, a "portage railroad" over the mountains, and a canal to Pittsburgh. That portage railroad used inclined
planes and stationary engines to haul canal boats, in sections, over the
mountains. Although the costs of building and operating the canal exceeded the revenues collected, it did do a considerable business; however, it never became a serious competitor to the Erie. Only four years
after the Mainline had been completed, a movement began to replace it
by a railroad. The threat of competition from the Baltimore and Ohio
Railroad led to the chartering of the Pennsylvania Railroad in 1846.
That railroad was built without any state aid, but it received more than
half its financing from subscriptions by local governments, especially
from the City of Philadelphia and the County of Allegheny (which contained the cities of Pittsburgh and Allegheny). By the end of 1852, the
railroad stretched from Philadelphia to Pittsburgh.

Meanwhile, there was activity in Baltimore. In 1823 Virginia granted
a charter for a canal to be built along the Potomac River from Georgetown to Cumberland, but it was stipulated that the charter had to be
confirmed by Maryland before it could go into effect. However, Maryland declined to go along, because the merchants of Baltimore were concerned that the project would aid Georgetown more than Baltimore.
That opposition was overcome, though, with the completion of the Erie
Canal and the beginning of the Pennsylvania project, and the ensuing
fear on the part of Baltimore that it might be shut out of the western
trade if something was not done. The original idea was to build a canal
from Baltimore that was to connect with this Chesapeake and Ohio Canal at Georgetown. But this plan was abandoned, and in 1827 it was
decided to build a railroad from Baltimore to the Ohio River. This was
a bold decision, since at that time the railroad was a new and relatively
untested means of transportation. By May of 1830 there were thirteen
miles in operation. At first the cars were drawn by horses, but steam
locomotives were adopted in 1831. This railroad, the Baltimore and
Ohio, reached the Ohio River at Wheeling in 1852.

Boston faced more obstacles in establishing a transportation link to the west than did the other Atlantic ports, since its only hope was to connect with the Hudson River at the eastern end of the Erie Canal. New York, of course, had the great advantage here, since the trade of the Erie was connected to that city by means of the wide and easily navigable Hudson River, while the best Boston could do was to hope to siphon off some of that trade by means of an expensive canal or railroad over the Berkshires. Nonetheless, a commission formed to investigate the possibility of building a canal reported in favor of the project in January 1826, although it pointed out that it probably would be necessary to dig a tunnel through the mountains. The Massachusetts legislature was dubious of the success of this project and delayed taking action. By 1827 the idea of a canal was abandoned, and it was decided to build a railroad, although work on it did not begin until 1837, and it was not until 1841 that a rail connection was completed between Boston and Albany. Rail construction from Boston now proceeded rapidly, and by 1850 there were lines connecting that city with Portland, Montreal, Albany, and New York. For a short time, Boston was the largest railroad center in the United States.

While all this railroad building activity was going on creating western links for Philadelphia, Baltimore, and Boston, New York's citizens were not sitting idle. Although the Erie Canal continued to be a profitable means for moving goods and people between east and west, the citizens of New York moved along with technology and competition. By 1851 two railroad lines crossed New York State connecting New York City with Lake Erie.

Transportation developments also were extremely important to the growth of western cities. The largest of these were located near a river, and so the introduction of the steamboat was of great significance. Before the steamboat made its appearance, it was relatively easy to ship goods downstream and reach an outlet to the sea through New Orleans. But the rapid currents of the Mississippi made upstream shipment very difficult, time consuming, and costly. The first major up-river trip by a steamboat was made in 1815, and by 1830 the steamboat had captured a monopoly of the passenger traffic and carried most upstream freight. The time of travel was greatly reduced by the steamboat, and so, too, was the cost of transportation. The average freight rates per ton-mile were reduced from $1.30 downstream or $5.80 upstream in 1816 to $.37 for either trip in 1860.

The steamboat was extremely important to the economy of Louisville. As early as 1829 more than a thousand steamboats were stopping at Louisville annually. Pittsburgh was not only a major steamboat port, but it also became the West's leading builder of those vessels, producing an estimated half of them. Cincinnati also profited greatly as a result of the steamboat, which was the main factor in that city's nearly 300 percent population increase in the 1820s. Like Pittsburgh, Cincinnati also built many steamboats. St. Louis more than doubled its trade with New Orleans with the advent of the steamboat. St. Louis became the distributing center for the entire upper-Mississippi region. It was there that goods were transferred from the comparatively deep water boats of the lower Mississippi to those of shallower draft that sailed the upper Mississippi and the Missouri. New Orleans, at the mouth of the Mississippi, obviously reaped great benefit from the development of the steamboat, and it soon registered more of them than any other American city. Even after western trade began moving eastward over canals, the value of goods received at New Orleans from the interior nearly doubled every decade between 1820 and 1860. It is important to note, though, that New Orleans was receiving more and more cotton but less and less wheat. Clearly, the output of the farms in the northern portion of the Mississippi Valley increasingly were moving eastward.

Also important to the growth of western cities was the building of canals. Most western cities became involved in the canal-building boom of the 1820s and '30s. Ohio was especially active in the construction of canals, and the cities of that state received great benefit from this. The principal object was to connect the Ohio River and Lake Erie. Two of the more important of these canals were the Ohio and Erie, which linked Cleveland with the Ohio River, and the Miami and Erie, which linked Cincinnati with Toledo. Another important canal, the Ohio and Pennsylvania, joined the Ohio River near Pittsburgh with the Ohio and Erie, and thus formed a connection between the Ohio canals and the Pennsylvania canal system. The Ohio River played a role in canal construction that developed from a rivalry between two cities. Cincinnati citizens were concerned about the control of river traffic by Louisville by virtue of its location at the Falls of the Ohio. They hoped to end that dominance by building a canal around the falls. It was clear that a proposal to build a canal in Kentucky could be blocked by Louisville, so they decided to advocate digging a canal on the Indiana side of the river. Louisville, fearful that such a canal would jeopardize its position, tried unsuccessfully to forestall interest in its construction. Since it was likely that a canal would be built, Louisville decided that it would be better to have it on the Kentucky side, and so they managed to get the Kentucky legislature to incorporate the Louisville and Portland Canal Company in 1825. As it turned out, the canal added to Louisville's prosperity. Another significant canal was the Illinois and Michigan Canal, which was very important to the development of Chicago. This canal, which was begun in 1836, connected Lake Michigan with the Illinois River, and thus with the Mississippi. Political pressure was brought to bear to secure a federal land grant to subsidize the building of this canal, which was completed in 1848.

These western canals and their linkage to those in the eastern states formed an extensive all-water communications system and greatly facilitated the movement of goods. But canals also had their drawbacks. Canals could not be built everywhere, they were expensive to construct, they needed a constant supply of water, they froze in the winter, and they were a slow means of transportation. Western cities, like those in the East, saw the railroad as a means of greatly increasing their prosperity. They set about promoting railroad construction with tremendous enthusiasm.

By 1857 Cincinnati had rail connections with the East and with St. Louis The city of Cincinnati had played a major role in obtaining these connections and had attempted to promote other rail link-ups. St. Louis also was active in promoting railroad construction. Hoping to become the principal terminus of a projected railway to the Pacific, the city and county of St. Louis had provided $2,200,000 to that railroad, as well as having made significant investments in other lines. Lexington, lacking a river location, expressed a very early interest in railroads, and subscribed to the stock of several that were considered beneficial to the city's commercial position. Wheeling, which was slated to be the western terminus of the Baltimore and Ohio, wanted to make sure the railroad got there, and so subscribed $500,000 to its stock. To increase the value of its rail connection, Wheeling decided to build a bridge over the Ohio River. Pittsburgh realized the bridge would give Wheeling an advantage, and so opposed its construction, making the claim that it would interfere with steamboat navigation. A bitter legal battle ensued that found its way to the United States Supreme Court.

The Gulf cities of Mobile and New Orleans invested substantially in railroad development. The citizens of Mobile voted to impose a heavy tax on themselves to raise money to invest in the Mobile and Ohio Railroad, and Mobile businessmen were active in securing aid from other sources. It became clear to the citizens of New Orleans that railroads were threatening the supremacy of the Mississippi, and so the city subscribed to nearly $5 million of railroad stock.

The cities of the Great Lakes region also were extremely active in railroad promotion, but none was more at the center of railroad building activity than Chicago. The first railroad of importance built in Illinois was the Galena and Chicago Union Railroad, which by 1855 had established a connection with the Mississippi. Many other railroad lines were built out of Chicago during the 1850s, among them the Chicago, Burlington and Quincy, the Chicago, Alton and St. Louis, and the Chicago and Rock Island. But of most importance to Chicago was the Illinois Central. This was a north-south line that joined Chicago and Cairo. The promoters of this railroad, which was to traverse a thinly-settled region, were convinced that it could be built only if the federal government provided aid. With the support of Senator Stephen A. Douglas, Congress ultimately granted land to Illinois to be used for the construction of the railroad. As a result, the Illinois Central received a right of way for the tracks as well as a substantial amount of land on either side of the right of way. In 1851 construction began in both Cairo and Chicago, and by 1856 both cities were linked by rail. By 1860, Chicago was the nation's leading railroad center, and these railroads greatly stimulated the growth of this city. Almost all of the important lines ran into Chicago and, significantly, none of them were through roads. Chicago citizens had been successful in preventing any road from building through or around the city.

The railroads not only were important to the growth of Chicago, they also contributed to urban growth throughout Illinois. The Illinois Central, in particular, was very active in townsite promotion. The towns established by the Illinois Central were widely advertised, and the railroad made considerable profit from the sale of town lots. Additionally, these towns helped build up traffic for the line, as well as increasing the value of nearby agricultural lands. It is not surprising, then, that there was considerable urban development along the route of that railroad. The Census of 1850 listed only ten towns, while in 1860 there were forty-seven, and by 1870 there were eighty-one. The population of these towns, excluding Chicago, increased from twelve thousand in 1850 to seventy thousand in 1860, and to 172 thousand by 1870.

The Development of Manufacturing. Although commerce played the leading role in American urban development prior to 1860, the importance of manufacturing should not be discounted. Cities were important to the growth of manufacturing in America. In the cities could be found concentrations of potential workers as well as ready markets for the products of industry. Good transportation was essential for the development of manufacturing and, as has been noted, cities played an important role in promoting the expansion of transportation. Furthermore, much of the financing for manufacturing enterprises came from city merchants who sought lucrative investments. Likewise, manufacturing encouraged urban development. New towns grew up at the sites of new industries, and older commercial centers grew further as a result of factory establishment.

Among the nation's largest cities, only New Orleans and Baltimore were almost entirely commercial. In New York 11 percent of the population was engaged in manufacturing pursuits in 1860, and the figure was nearly the same for Boston. Philadelphia was an important manufacturing center, with 17.5 percent of its population employed in that area. Cincinnati was becoming almost as important as an industrial center as it was a commercial city, with 18 percent of its residents engaged in manufacturing by 1860. A similar percentage was so employed in Pittsburgh. Other cities were already becoming primarily manufacturing centers, such as Newark (26 percent of its population was engaged in manufacturing), Lowell (36 percent), and Lynn (45 percent).

New England benefited more than any other section from the rise of new towns, and this was a major reason why New England became the most highly urbanized section of the country. Since early machinery was operated by water power, factory towns tended to develop at points where the power was available, and New England had many swift-flowing streams. Thus, Lynn became a leading shoe and boot manufacturing center, and Lowell became a leader in textile manufacturing. Lowell played a particularly interesting role in the development of manufacturing in the United States. It was founded by Boston merchants at a site a short distance from that well-established port city. With labor in short supply, they decided to tap an underutilized source—the daughters of New England farmers. They attracted them to this factory town by providing clean and airy workplaces and supervised dormitories. Because at first the machinery was powered by water, Lowell avoided the griminess associated with factory towns. Soon, Lowell was seen as a model factory town, and it was a site to be seen by visitors from abroad. (*See Document No. 6.*) Before long, though, steam became the source of power and the farmers' daughters were replaced by Irish immigrants, and Lowell was no longer regarded as the ideal industrial environment.

In the major northeastern seaport cities manufacturing increasingly added to the economy. In addition to the longstanding shipbuilding and outfitting industries of these cities, they became important producers of clothing. The clothing industry, even this early, was at the forefront of New York's manufacturing activity, but characteristic of New York was the large variety of industrial activities. Philadelphia, too, produced significant quantities of clothing, boots, and shoes, but it also was known for its large iron industry and its highly advanced machine tool and locomotive plants. Among southern cities, Richmond was the only one that stood out as a manufacturing center. It was a significant producer of iron and iron products, and flour milling and tobacco manufacturing also were important to the city's economy. Among western cities, Pittsburgh already was beginning to emerge as an industrial city. Pittsburgh's iron industry started at the beginning of the nineteenth century and it grew steadily. The production of glass was another activity that had early roots in Pittsburgh. Before this period was over, Cincinnati led the nation in pork-product production. While local boosters dubbed Cincinnati "The Queen City," others referred to it as "Porkopolis." Interestingly, assembly-line production may have had its origins in the pork-packing houses of Cincinnati. Other important industries in that city were machinery manufacturing, woodworking, whiskey distilling, and flour milling. (*See Document No. 7.*) The younger cities of the Great Lakes region were beginning to develop manufacturing activities that later were to characterize them. In Chicago, for example, the meat-packing industry grew rapidly, and by 1861 that city was packing more hogs than Cincinnati. As rail connections provided Chicago with a vast agricultural hinterland, the manufacture of agricultural implements became increasingly important. Chicago's position as a rail center also led to the manufacture of iron products for the railroads, as well as locomotive production.

The People of the Cities. The foreign-born made up a significant element of the urban population during this period, and they represented a greater percentage of the urban population than that of the nation as a whole. While by 1860 the foreign-born comprised 15 percent of the population of the United States, in several major cities they accounted for between 50 and 60 percent of the inhabitants.

During this period immigrants came mostly from northern and western Europe, and the Irish and the Germans were the most numerous. The Irish predominated in the seaport cities and the manufacturing cities of New England, while the Germans usually were the most numerous foreign-born residents of the cities of the interior waterways. The cities of the Mississippi Valley had a very high incidence of foreign-born, while the percentages in southern cities were fairly low. A port that was known to have good access to a further destination would be favored by the immigrant. Also important was the number of people of a particular nationality already in that port. Immigration laws, which were local rather than national, were another factor, and jobs and living conditions also were considerations. Still another factor, especially for the poorest of immigrants, was the incidence of shipping to a port.

Immigrants from Ireland made the most pronounced impact on the American city between 1830 and 1860. By 1865 there were 2.5 million Irish-born people in the United States. The great proportion of them tended to disperse themselves among the most highly urbanized sections of the United States. Driven out of Ireland by poverty and famine, the Irish, as a group, were among the poorest immigrants to come to America; and because they lacked the funds necessary to move westward, they concentrated in the eastern cities. Some did leave the eastern cities, but usually only when they were recruited by contractors for internal improvement projects. For the most part, the Irish were employed in the least desirable occupations, working primarily as heavy laborers or servants. In the cities they commonly worked as longshoremen or in the construction industry. They also found employment as domestic servants and as servants and waiters in hotels.

The Irish were a very important element in New York, where most of them lived in the city's worst slums. They were particularly numerous in the region known as the Five Points, perhaps the most notorious slum in America. Irish men comprised a majority of the city's heavy labor population, and about a quarter of the Irish men and women worked as household laborers. Most of New York's hotel workers seem to have been Irish, and the majority of cab drivers also were Irish. Some of New York's Irish inhabitants became small businessmen, particularly as proprietors of saloons. The Irish were beginning to discover police work as an occupation. By 1855 a third of New York's police force was foreign born, and three-quarters of that group were Irish. New York's Irish and black residents competed for jobs as domestic servants, waiters in hotels, and longshoreman. But skin color was an important factor, and the Irish usually won out and got the better-paying jobs. This struggle for employment was one reason for conflict between Irish and blacks, but racial prejudice should not be discounted, nor should employers' frequent use of blacks as strikebreakers.

In Boston the Irish were more influential than they were in New York. The Irish constituted the overwhelming majority of Boston's foreign-born population. Boston was a particularly inhospitable city to immigrants, and so for years they avoided settling there. But the Irish had few choices. They left for America on the cheapest and most frequent sailings, and these frequently brought them to Boston. On arrival in that city, their poverty prevented them from moving elsewhere. As in New York, the Irish in Boston inhabited the least desirable areas of the city, and they were crowded into the poorest housing. Also, as in New York, Boston's Irish mostly were employed as unskilled laborers and as domestic servants. The availability of cheap Irish labor, especially that of women, contributed to the development of a ready-made clothing industry in Boston. The presence of a labor surplus, especially during the 1850s, was important to the industrialization of New England. In Boston, as elsewhere, there was considerable hostility between Irish and black residents.

For the most part, the Irish were not very numerous in the cities of the South; nonetheless, the Irish population was of some importance in several southern cities. This certainly was the case in New Orleans, the only southern city with a large immigrant population. In 1860 New Orleans had more than 24,000 Irish-born residents, representing about 15 percent of the city's total population. Considering New Orleans' reputation for being an unhealthy place, and the existence of an extremely anti-immigrant Know-Nothing party in that city, only the lack of resources to move elsewhere would keep the Irish there. In New Orleans, as elsewhere, they found employment as heavy laborers, cab drivers, and waiters in hotels. In each of these occupations they replaced both free blacks and slaves, who formerly had been the dominant workers.

In the western cities the Irish almost always were outnumbered by the Germans; still, they constituted a significant element of the western urban population by 1860. Cincinnati, for example, had more than nineteen thousand Irish residents by that year. Most of them were involved in heavy labor and as porters and waiters in hotels. In Chicago, construction of the Illinois and Michigan Canal attracted Irish workers, who accounted for more then 20 percent of the city's population by 1850. Not surprisingly, Chicago's Irish workers were found mainly in jobs requiring little skill, such as heavy laborers, teamsters, and domestic servants. They lived in the least desirable areas of the city, primarily the North Side and the slaughterhouse district.

The migration of Germans to America was motivated by similar reasons to those of the Irish; the primary cause was economic. Another motivation, though, may be found in the disturbed political conditions of western Europe, particularly in the German states. The Germans usually were financially better off than were the Irish, and they were more specifically pulled to the land. Nevertheless, a considerable number settled in the cities. This was partly because many of them lacked the resources to take up farming, while others preferred to be among their own people. Many Germans remained in the eastern cities, but thousands moved into the Mississippi Valley. As was noted before, the western cities were more marked by German migration than were the eastern cities. Because there were a great many skilled artisans among the Germans, their migration made a very important contribution to the industrial development of many of these western cities.

The Germans constituted a large and distinctive group in New York during this period, since that city contained more German-born residents than any other city in the United States. The Germans, more than the Irish, tended to congregate together, so that there was a separate German section in New York. Not only did they enjoy better living conditions, for the most part, than did the Irish, they also held better jobs. While most Irish immigrants were laborers and servants, only 5 percent of employed Germans were laborers and 10 percent servants. They were numerous as workers in New York's growing ready-made clothing industry, and they constituted the majority of upholsterers and cabinet makers, as well as dominating in the manufacturing of pianos.

Because New York's port was favored by so many of the ships crossing from Europe, the other Atlantic Coast cities received far fewer German immigrants. That was true even for Philadelphia, especially considering that Germans had settled in that city since the early eighteenth century. The only southern city to receive any substantial number of German migrants was New Orleans; though most of those moved on to take up settlement in the Mississippi Valley or in Texas. Some, though, remained in the Crescent City, which by 1860 had a German population of nearly twenty thousand.

The cities of the American West were especially noted for their German-born residents, which, while fewer in number than in New York, represented sizable proportions of the populations of many of those cities. Cincinnati, quite early, became one of the most important German-American cities, with the German-born population representing more than a quarter of the total. In St. Louis the German-population was even more substantial; better than one out of every three St. Louis residents was German. The cities of the Great Lakes region also were receiving large number of German migrants. Many of the earlier migrants headed west by way of the Erie Canal, and substantial numbers settled in Buffalo, at the western end of the canal. Germans began to move to Chicago in the 1830s, and by 1860 they accounted for 20 percent of Chicago's population. A substantial majority of Chicago's German population worked in manufacturing, with fewer than a third of them as unskilled laborers. In fact, there were more skilled workers among the Germans than among any other nationality group in Chicago. Between 1840 and 1860 many Germans settled in Wisconsin, and Milwaukee became the distributing center for these settlers. By 1860 approximately two-thirds of Milwaukee's large foreign-born population was of German origin.

Clearly, this large influx of foreign-born migrants to the United States created a number of problems for the nation. Because so many of them were poor, the problem of welfare was aggravated. Not all Americans welcomed them, and that led to political tensions, which were manifested most specifically in the Nativist movement. Differences in customs led to social tensions, and competition for jobs created economic tensions. On balance, though, the contributions made by the foreign-born outweighed these problems. The most obvious contribution was the addition to the population, creating a large domestic market for the products of agriculture and industry. They also contributed the hard labor that was necessary to build the nation, its cities, and its internal improvements, as well as the skills to help build an emerging industrial power. America's religious pattern was changed and diversified as a result of immigration, which also added new tastes and practices to the urban culture.

While the conventional view of the black population of the United States in the years before 1860 is that of slaves working on southern plantations, slaves and free blacks also resided in the cities of the South and the North. While their numbers were not as great as those of European immigrants, they nonetheless comprised a group of significant size and importance.

The black populations of cities in the north usually were strictly segregated. For the most part, they also held the least desirable jobs and occupied inferior and overcrowded housing. Boston, not being a major station on the underground railway and with limited economic opportunities, attracted few people of African descent. New York's numbers were somewhat larger. Its black population increased from 10,886 in 1820 to 16,358 by 1840, primarily as a result of migration. But by 1850 the number had declined to 13,815, and by 1860 to 12,581. Increasingly severe restrictions placed upon slaves in the South made freedom very difficult to attain, and so there were fewer free blacks available to migrate. Furthermore, following the passage of the Fugitive Slave Act in 1850 runaway slaves were more likely to go to Canada than to the northern states. Also adding to this decline in population was the fact that the death rate was high among New York's black residents. Before 1860 New York's black population did not live in any specific area, but was distributed throughout the city. Nonetheless, they did live in segregated areas, even though those districts were not very large. The largest occupational group among New York's blacks was domestic service, next came laborers, and then waiters and laundresses. In each of these occupations, though, they gradually were being replaced by Irish workers. They also frequently were employed as barbers and private coachmen. Throughout the period blacks in New York were segregated from whites in most activities. Black children were educated in separate schools, and far less money was spent on those schools than on those for white children. (*See Document No. 8.*) New York also had a separate orphan asylum for black children. Blacks could not ride the same omnibuses or street railway cars as whites. Even in prison black and white were separated; and here, too, the accommodations for blacks were inferior. Life for black residents of Philadelphia was no better. That city, with a black population of 22,000 in 1860, contained more black residents than any other northern city. As in New York, living conditions were horrible and employment was primarily in menial occupations, and, of course, blacks were strictly segregated from whites. Racial prejudice appears to have been very strong in Philadelphia, where there were five major anti-black riots between 1832 and 1849.

Even a casual perusal of population data for southern cities reveals a very interesting trend: By 1860 the institution of slavery was declining in those cities. In every southern city the percentage of slaves had declined by 1860. Fewer southern city dwellers owned slaves in that year, and their holdings were smaller. Additionally, female slaves outnumbered male slaves. These trends were not occurring in the rural regions. There, slavery, rather than going into a decline, seems to have been doing better than ever. It would seem, then, that something in the urban environment was hostile to slavery. One of the most significant factors contributing to the decline of urban slavery was the difficulty of controlling slaves in an urban environment, and the success of the slave system in the United States depended upon absolute control of the slaves. A popular work system that developed helped contribute to this breakdown of control. Because the slave owner frequently had more slaves than were necessary for the owner's business and domestic activities, the master often hired out the slaves to others who needed their labor. Sometimes, the slave was encouraged to find his own employment, and then periodically return a certain sum of money to the master. Living conditions also contributed to this breakdown of authority. In addition to permitting their slaves to find employment, some masters found it convenient or profitable to permit their slaves to find their own housing. This practice actually was prohibited by law in southern cities, but the laws were not enforced effectively. Clearly, these two practices gave urban slaves a measure of freedom not enjoyed by their rural counterparts. Then, too, since there were no black ghettos in the southern cities, slaves lived surrounded by free blacks and whites, and opportunities thus existed for fraternization with the non-slave population. Although the education of slaves usually was prohibited by law, such laws were very difficult to enforce in the urban environment. Since cities were on the main lines of communication, it also was easier for urban slaves to run away than it was for those residing on plantations. Those slaves who violated laws would be apprehended by city authorities, who also would mete out punishments. The absolute authority of the master, so necessary to the maintenance of the slave system, was thus diminished. Because urban slaves were taking on so many attributes of freedom it became difficult to distinguish slaves from free blacks, and so color became emphasized more than legal status. A result of that was that a pattern of rigid segregation of white and black developed.

The Urban Scene. The growth in the population of America's cities gave rise to changes in their size and physical appearance as a result of the necessity of accommodating the new urban dwellers. Not only the size of the population, but also its nature, affected the physical appearance of a city. Thus, the influx of poor immigrants led to an increase in the number of shabby dwellings. On the other hand, the increasing numbers who were prospering from developments in commerce and industry also had to be housed, and their dwellings obviously would be more substantial and more attractive than those of the poor. Commerce and industry also directly affected the appearance of American cities. Buildings were erected to house the various industries; but more important during this era were the buildings devoted to commerce. Buildings to house the offices of firms and buildings to house the products of commerce were erected at a furious pace in the bustling commercial cities. Developments in commerce and transportation brought a greatly increased number of transients to the cities, and these people, no less than the city's permanent residents, had to be housed. Thus, the era of the great American urban hotel began. Along with this came an increase in the number of restaurants. Shops increased in number, size, and variety. The facilities for culture and entertainment, traditionally centered in the cities, were generally expanded, although they were rarely supported by public funds.

An increasingly noticeable characteristic of urban life that became important during these years was the tendency toward specialization. Specialization came about primarily as a result of the large number of people who lived in the cities. A glance at the shops in the large cities revealed this trend. The specialty store was supplanting the general store, and the luxury emporium was making its appearance. Specialization also was apparent in religious facilities, educational facilities, cultural facilities, entertainment facilities, and in the availability of professional services.

Population growth led to the physical expansion of America's cities. The older cities, in planning their newer areas usually used Philadel-

phia's checkerboard plan, and most of the newer cities had been laid out
this way from the beginning. Although the city streets of this era were
often filthy and badly paved, they frequently presented an attractive appearance, partly as a result of the common custom of planting trees on
either side. Yet in busy commercial cities, such as Boston and New York,
some of the best streets were marred by unattractive telegraph wires
strung on unpainted poles. The extraordinary commercial activity of
New York was evident in its streets. Although in the 1850s the city vir-
tually ended at 42nd Street, the streets were laid out and numbered at
least as far as 150th Street. A walk through the streets of New York made
it evident that this was a busy, bustling metropolis. The roadways were
jammed with vehicles of all sizes and descriptions, and pedestrians had
to take particular care to keep out of their way. The sidewalks were just
as crowded with people, but they also often were encumbered with
boxes, crates, and merchandise belonging to the various shops. The
longest, busiest, and most important street in New York was Broadway,
which was lined with shops, restaurants, hotels, and commercial structures. The main street for bankers and brokers was Wall Street, and the
most fashionable residential street for New York's wealthier citizens was
Fifth Avenue. Despite the imposing plan for the nation's capital, Washington's streets still had a straggling and unfinished appearance by
1860. There were some rows of handsome buildings in the vicinity of
the Capitol, but only a short distance away the number of buildings began to decrease rapidly. One of the most visually attractive cities was
Charleston, where streets lined with magnolias and palmettos produced
an almost tropical appearance. Western cities were less distinctive, but
were notable for broad, tree-lined streets following a rectangular pattern.

Urban growth was outward rather than upward. There were no really
tall buildings erected during this period; the tallest were only five or six
stories high. What stood out on the skyline were church steeples. While
this was not a great era in urban architecture, several cities could boast
of handsome public buildings; but these were mainly to be found in the
cities of the east coast, from Washington northward. The South had few
large public buildings, and western cities were mostly too new to excel
in this area. There were many new commercial structures erected during these years to house the rapidly growing businesses located in the

downtown areas. The best examples of these were in New York. Some architectural and engineering innovations were made during the latter part of this period. Most notable among these was the use of cast iron for building construction. Cast iron offered many advantages. It permitted rapid construction, since the building elements would be cast in a factory and then bolted together at the building site. The material was strong and thus permitted large windows for better interior lighting, and it also was fire retardant. The iron usually was cast in classical forms, and the buildings were painted to imitate limestone or marble. These buildings were very popular, and many were erected in the commercial districts of New York and other cities. It was also during this period that the elevator made its appearance, which would make it feasible to erect taller buildings in the future. The first practical passenger elevator was installed in a cast-iron building in New York in 1857.

The increasing numbers of well-to-do urban dwellers lived in attractive, comfortable houses. These house varied in style from city to city, depending upon the city's origins, its age, its climate, and the wealth of its inhabitants, among other factors; but each city had at least one street or section that contained some fine houses. In the crowded cities of the Northeast, the houses usually were built of brick or stone and, except for some very large houses on the fringes of the cities, typically were attached to each other. Gardens rarely were seen. But in the South and the West, houses more commonly were built of wood and stood alone surrounded by their own plots of land. The interiors of the better houses, reflecting the prosperity of their owners, were expensively and ornately furnished. (*See Document No. 9.*) The homes of less-wealthy citizens seldom were described by contemporaries, and few illustrations exist. Generally, artisans lived in small brick or wooden houses, while the poor lived in shacks or were crowded into dilapidated tenements.

Among the largest buildings in most cities were the hotels. Developments in transportation resulted in the need to accommodate more transients. Although catering primarily to travelers, these hotels also housed many bachelors as well as married couples who did not wish to set up housekeeping. The first American luxury hotel was the Tremont House in Boston, which opened in the fall of 1829. By 1860, fine hotels could be found in almost every city. The larger cities offered the visitor a variety of hotels from which to choose, but even cities on the edge of the frontier were likely to have at least one fine hotel. The size and luxuriousness of these establishments made a profound impression upon travelers from abroad. One English visitor wrote that an American hotel "would supply a regiment with beds." The hotels in major cities, he noted, were "as large as any two of our club-houses fused together, as roomy as Buckingham palace, and not much inferior to a palace in its internal fittings."[5] While there was a certain variation in hotel rates, the average, by the 1850s, seems to have been $2 per day. The guest received quite a bit for this charge. Not only did he or she get a comfortable room to sleep in, but also was permitted to use the sumptuously appointed drawing-, reading-, and smoking-rooms. In addition, all meals in the hotel dining-room were included in this fee. (*See Document No. 10.*)

Many American cities contained a number of fine shops that offered urban dwellers a wide selection of domestic and imported items. It should not be surprising that New York, the most important commercial center in the United States, led all other cities in the number, variety, and quality of its retail establishments. Some of the Empire City's shops occupied their own buildings, but most were located on the street level of hotels and other public buildings. New York's dry-goods shops were especially famous. The largest and best known of these was A. T. Stewart's, which was housed in a five-story, white marble building just north of City Hall. But even in the newer western cities, shoppers could purchase a wide variety of products of American and European industry.

Most cities contained several eating establishments in addition to hotel dining rooms, but New York clearly was the leading city for restaurants. The best known New York eating establishments were Taylor's, Thomson's, and Delmonico's. Taylor's, especially, was a large, ornate establishment, particularly famous for its ice cream and ices. A popular type of eating place in New York throughout this period was the "oyster saloon," of which there were many in the city. They usually were located in the basements of commercial buildings, and they catered to the New Yorker's passion for eating oysters, which were served in every conceivable form. Even Washington, which during these years appeared to be a rather "raw" city, had its share of fine restaurants. And San Francisco,

[5] Walter Thornbury, *Criss-Cross Journeys,* 2 vols. (London: Hurst and Blackett, 1873), 2:101.

a late arrival on the urban scene, was singled out for its restaurants, especially one that featured the novelty of Chinese cuisine.

The cities also contained many places where both citizens and visitors could spend their leisure hours. From dance halls and saloons, to
museums, theaters, and concert halls, there were places where people,
no matter what their tastes, could find entertainment.

The inhabitants of New York had available to them a greater variety
of entertainment facilities than could be found in any other city in the
United States. While entertainment facilities were found throughout
the city, they were most heavily concentrated in the vicinity of Broadway. Among the lower classes, New York's numerous saloons were very
popular, and another type of establishment low on the scale of accept-
ability was the dance hall. One of the most conspicuous of New York's
attractions was Barnum's Museum, which was located on Broadway
near City Hall. The exterior of the building was covered with large
paintings of animals and birds. Projecting from the walls at frequent
intervals were flagpoles, from which brightly-colored banners flapped in
the wind; and on a balcony over the entrance was a noisy, and not very
musical, brass band. For the most part the interior fulfilled the promise
made by the display outside the museum. Badly-executed wax figures,
paintings of famous Americans, stuffed animals and birds, live animals,
"freaks of nature," and a weird assortment of other items were on display. In addition to performing its function as a museum of sorts, Barnum's also housed a small theater that was a popular attraction. Theater
was a major source of entertainment for New Yorkers, and some of the
leading actors, singers, and dancers of Europe and America performed
in them. Before the mid-1840s opera was not especially popular in New
York. The first season of Italian opera began in November 1825; however in the 'thirties and early 'forties operas were performed only spo-
radically. In the early 1850s Castle Garden, at the southern tip of Manhattan island was New York's principal opera house, but in 1854 the
Academy of Music was erected on Fourteenth Street at Irving Place.
This large, elaborately decorated building remained the home of opera
in New York until the erection of the Metropolitan Opera House in
1883. From 1853–1858 the Crystal Palace, located on Sixth Avenue at
Forty-second Street was one of the sights of New York. Originally constructed to house the first world's fair in America, this iron and glass
structure later was used, off and on, for a variety of purposes, such as

celebrations and exhibitions. It burned to the ground in 1858 in one of New York's most spectacular fires.

In Philadelphia similar forms of entertainment could be found, though on a smaller scale. Like New York, Philadelphia had its saloons and dives; and like New York, Philadelphia had a Barnum's Museum. By the 1850s the Quaker City probably had as many as five theaters. In Boston, however, the respectability of theatrical performances continued to be doubted by the city fathers until well into the nineteenth century. Nevertheless, theatrical performances could be seen in Boston, and they were well attended. The would-be theater-goer might not enter a building called a theater, though. Instead, that person might go into the Boston Museum, walk rapidly past the stuffed birds and other curios to the rear of the building. There, in an auditorium could be witnessed a "theatrical exhibition." However, soon one would not have to resort to such subterfuges. In 1836 the National Theater was built, and in 1854 the Boston Theater, with a reputed seating capacity of 3,000, was opened. One of the most popular forms of entertainment in Boston was the public lecture, and lectures were given on almost every conceivable subject. They were popular in other cities, too, but they were received with the greatest enthusiasm by Bostonians.

From society balls to low-class dance halls, New Orleans offered the full spectrum of mid-nineteenth-century entertainment. At Mardi Gras time, New Orleans, then as now was at the height of its gaiety, and balls, parades, and universal merry-making abounded. The city's several gambling casinos were very popular, and one of the Crescent City's best-known entertainment industries was prostitution. The theater was fairly popular. In 1850 three theaters were offering regular programs in the English language, and weekly performances in French were offered at the opera house. Theaters usually had regular orchestras and resident stock companies, but visiting stars were the main attractions. Opera was even more popular, and New Orleans was the first city in the United States to have a regular opera season. Opera in New Orleans was an important social institution, with attendance at Thursday and Saturday night performances a "must" for the social elite. Concerts frequently were given during the winter season. Most memorable were the thirteen concerts given by Jenny Lind in 1851, and two years later the pianist Louis Gottschalk captivated the Crescent City—especially its women.

The western cities usually contained entertainment facilities similar to those found in the East. However, the facilities were not usually as numerous, and, when it came to theatrical performances and similar types of entertainment, the quality was almost always inferior. The rapid growth of the nation's transportation system, particularly the railroad, made it possible for noted stars of the stage to travel to perform in western cities. Although they attracted substantial audiences, they usually had to perform with inferior local stock companies. In Pittsburgh, museums were among the most popular amusements. These museums contained the usual hodge-podge of odds and ends of curios and hoaxes, and, as in other cities, museums played host to "theatrical exhibitions." Visiting circuses attracted large crowds. Travelers to Cincinnati as late as the 1850s, although impressed with the city's size and importance, considered it a very dull place as far as entertainment was concerned. But one western city that hardly could be called dull was San Francisco. Gambling and drinking apparently were the primary forms of amusement in 1850, and the city contained numerous saloons and gambling houses. As the decade wore on, though, theaters were built and other more "respectable" forms of entertainment began to appear.

Most cities had few places where a person wanting to escape the bustle of city streets could sit quietly. There were private, commercial parks in many cities in the early years; but most cities had few public parks, and what parks they had usually were too small. New York, for many years, had only Battery Park, at the tip of Manhattan Island, and the park surrounding City Hall. This clearly was not enough park space for a city with a population of more than 800,000. The citizens of Philadelphia and Boston were somewhat luckier than those of New York; Philadelphians had the beautiful Fairmount Park at the edge of the city, while Bostonians could take pride in the Common.

Because most cities had a shortage of parks, people often went to the nearby cemeteries for Sunday picnics. The first of these romantic so-called "rural cemeteries" was Mount Auburn in Cambridge, Massachusetts, which dates from 1831. Soon, most cities had similar cemeteries. The most famous of these were New York's Greenwood Cemetery (in Brooklyn), and Philadelphia's Laurel Hill Cemetery. The cemeteries of New Orleans scarcely took the place of parks, but they were certainly the most unusual in the United States, and were a major tourist attraction. The peculiarity of the New Orleans cemeteries was that the dead were placed in above-ground tombs rather than being buried, for in this low-lying area a grave could not be dug without it filling up with water.

It should be pointed out that although the cities were growing rapidly, they still were small enough to permit a Sunday drive, or perhaps a walk, to the country. Thus, New Yorkers might cross th Hudson and visit the Elysian Fields in Hoboken, New Jersey. But at the rate the cities were growing this could not continue much longer.

By 1850 in New York the agitation for a park reached the point where the creation of a park became an issue in the mayoralty campaign of that year. In 1853 the state legislature granted the city authorization to buy the land between 59th and 106th streets and Fifth and Eighth avenues, and acquisition of land began for what was to become Central Park. Frederick Law Olmsted was appointed Park Superintendent in 1857, and under his supervision the site began to be cleared. This was a difficult job, since the area really was a mess, and there were perhaps as many as three hundred squatters on the land, whom the police had to eject. Also in 1857, it was announced that a $2,000 prize would be granted for the best design for the park. Originally, Olmsted had no intention of entering this contest, until Calvert Vaux, an architect, suggested they collaborate on a plan. Their plan, which was known as "Greensward," was chosen as the best, and Olmsted was appointed Architect-in-Chief of the park. New York's Central Park was to be an inspiration for the creation of parks in many other cities, and Olmsted became the premier landscape designer in the United States.

The Development of Urban Services. For the most part, the municipalities provided little in the way of services for the city dweller; services either were not performed at all, or they were performed by volunteer organizations or by private commercial companies. Nevertheless, there was some evidence of cities assuming responsibility for a limited number of services. One reason for slowness along these lines was that most people believed that governments should not take on functions that could be fulfilled by private enterprise.

A walk through the streets of most cities made the lack of urban services readily apparent. The larger American cities usually had paved streets, but the pavements were not always in good condition. Moreover, the streets were not clean; indeed, with few exceptions, they were filthy. Stone or macadamized roadways were rare, and where they did exist, they frequently were in a poor state of repair. Most city streets in the

United States either were unpaved, or were covered with wooden planks. Municipalities, for the most part, did not provide for the cleaning of streets. If a street was swept at all it probably was a result of the street's occupants paying someone to do the job. Nature frequently helped out by providing rain to wash the dirt away. In many cities animal scavengers eliminated some of the garbage. Sewerage systems, when they existed at all, usually were inadequate, and often consisted of no more than open ditches running alongside the roadways.

New York's streets were mostly paved, but they were kept in a poor state of repair, and this was true even of Broadway. The streets also were very dirty. Before the 1850s some of the refuse in New York's streets was removed by the hordes of pigs that roamed about. This four-legged sanitation department, however, proved a mixed blessing, for the tough city pig made life hazardous for the city's human inhabitants. By the 1850s the pigs mostly had disappeared from New York's streets, but it was noticed that the rat population of the city was increasing. On the other hand, Philadelphia seems to have had reasonably well-paved streets that were kept comparatively clean. Philadelphia's brick pavements were somewhat unusual; but perhaps more unusual was that they were regularly washed, a practice made possible by the city's excellent water-supply system. However, Philadelphia still had many open sewers as late as the 1850s. Boston also seems to have had good pavements that were kept in excellent condition.

The cities of the South were noted for badly paved and filthy streets; but few cities anywhere seem to have been as disquietingly dirty as New Orleans. As late as 1860 an Englishwoman visiting New Orleans remarked, "we were almost suffocated with the fearful stench. Every street has its gutters filled with thick green slime which emits a most appalling effluvium. We were sickened by it."[6] (*See Document No. 11.*) Charleston had a unique, and apparently efficient, unofficial sanitation department that was made up of a number of turkey buzzards. These birds took on the self-imposed task of removing large quantities of debris from the streets. The city authorities obviously were not blind to the good services performed by the buzzards, for they imposed a fine of

---

[6] Disher, M. Willson, ed., *The Cowells in America: Being the Diary of Mrs. Sam Cowell During Her Husband's Concert Tour in the Years 1860–1861* (London: Oxford University press, 1934), 56.

several dollars upon anyone who wilfully killed one of them. (*See Document No. 12.*)

Neither street paving nor sanitary conditions were any better in western cities than elsewhere in the nation. In Pittsburgh some streets were paved with cobblestones, but for the most part the streets were seas of mud. Hogs, dogs, and rats roamed the streets. Encounters with unattended animals were not the only reasons why a walk through the streets of Pittsburgh was hazardous; shopkeepers used the streets as outdoor warehouses, stairs to cellars were uncovered, and the sewers were open. In the early days of most western cities most streets were unpaved. The first surfacing probably would consist of wooden planks. Holes and loose boards in the sidewalks were a danger to pedestrians, while in wet weather mud oozed up between the planks in the roadways and was thrown into the air by passing vehicles. Such was the type of surfacing used in Chicago, and in wet weather the streets were so muddy that they became the subject of local jokes. But by the 1850s the streets of that city were being altered. To improve drainage, they were being raised several feet above their original level. This ambitious undertaking gave the city a peculiar appearance. Visitors pointed out that a walk through the city consisted of ascending and descending steps between the old and the new levels. Instead of board coverings, the new sections of the streets had granite pavements.

Perhaps nothing is more important to urban life than an adequate water supply, and this period shows a trend toward replacing private sources of water with municipally owned waterworks. This began in 1799 when Philadelphia authorized the construction of the Fairmount Waterworks, which was completed in 1822 and provided Philadelphia with a dependable water supply. New York's first waterworks was constructed in 1829; but this was merely a reservoir to provide water for extinguishing fires—the water was not considered fit to drink. There was considerable agitation for a better water supply for New York. The leading proposal involved securing water from the Croton watershed, about forty miles upstate from the city. Legislation authorizing the project was passed in 1835, and in 1837 work began on the construction of a a dam on the Croton River. From the Croton dam a masonry aqueduct brought the water to the Harlem River, and it was carried across the river by way of the magnificent High Bridge. From there, the water was brought down Manhattan Island through pipes to a distributing reservoir on Fifth Avenue between Forty-first and Forty-second streets. This system was opened with great ceremony on July 4, 1842. The building of the Croton System was considered one of the great engineering achievements of its day. Boston authorized a municipal water system in 1844. On October 25, 1848 Boston's Cochituate Aqueduct was completed, and the city had a great celebration. During most of this period Washington households typically utilized spring water, which was carried by slaves from the wells in the public squares. Recommendations for a public water system had been made as early as 1830, but the necessary congressional approval was not obtained. However, when the Library of Congress burned in December of 1851, it became clear that a reliable water supply was necessary, if only to fight fires. In 1853 Congress voted to build a water system at government expense, and on January 3, 1859 that system first brought water to the city. During this period public water systems were established in Richmond, New Orleans, Cincinnati, Pittsburgh, St. Louis, and Chicago, among others. By 1860 the sixteen largest cities had some sort of waterworks, and twelve of these were municipally owned.

Even though fire remained an ever-present menace in these crowded cities, throughout this period most of them relied upon volunteer fire companies. Although these fire companies resisted attempts at professionalization, more complicated fire-fighting machinery helped bring about their downfall. The members of the volunteer fire departments usually were young men looking for excitement. The prized possession of each company was its engine, which was kept highly polished. At the sound of the alarm all the fire companies in the vicinity would race madly in the direction of the fire, and pedestrians were wise to get out of the way. To the first company at the scene of the fire would go the honor of extinguishing the flames. Should two companies arrive at the same time, a fight might break out over the question of which had arrived first. To be called out on a false alarm was a major disappointment to the firemen, and so on the way back they often would stop at a saloon for a few drinks, and the episode might well end in a brawl.

The early detection of fires was of great importance. In many cities a man was stationed at the top of a tall building to act as a lookout for fires. If smoke or flames were sighted an alarm was sounded, and the location of the fire would be indicated, which commonly was done by using a bell to toll out the number of the district. However, by the 1850s several cities had installed telegraphic systems for reporting fires. (*See Document No. 13.*)

At the beginning of the period police protection in most cities was poorly organized and impermanent. Only in the South, with its large slave population, was there any regularity or organization. In most cities one might have some difficulty in locating a policeman if the need arose. There were not very many of them, and they did not wear uniforms. They were identified only by a badge, usually made of copper (thus the origin of the term "cop" for a policeman), which could be concealed in time of trouble should the policeman desire to shirk his duty. By the 1830s most large northern cities found that increases in crime and disorder were greater than their police organizations could handle. These increases resulted from many factors: rapid economic and physical growth; increase in immigration and the tensions that brought about; crowding and inadequate housing for the growing populations; an increase in racial tensions. A series of riots in New York and elsewhere during the 1830s pointed up the need for efficient police protection. Lacking such a force, New York had to call for military aid during some riots in 1834. Very important to establishing a police force in New York was the passage in 1829 of the Peel Act in England, which provided for the regularization of the London police force. New York saw itself as the London of America, and so by 1836 New York's mayor was proposing the establishment of a London-style police for his city. But there was opposition from those who believed that a formal police was incompatible with American democratic institutions. However, an unsolved murder case in 1841 brought out that police officers would not work on a homicide unless they were promised substantial rewards, since their income came primarily from fees and rewards. In 1845 a standing day and night police force was established in New York. An attempt at that time to require the police to wear uniforms met with bitter opposition, and it was not until 1853 that a uniform was adopted. Similar developments were taking place in other cities in the Northeast.

In the western cities police protection was, if anything, worse than in the cities of the Northeast. In Pittsburgh, for example, day constables and night watchmen were organized as separate entities until 1868, and even then the combined forces only numbered 122 men. In Chicago, as late as 1855, there were only eighty policemen, and they did not wear uniforms until 1861. Milwaukee did not formally establish a police department unit 1855, and while uniforms were prescribed in 1859, police apparently did not wear them until 1874.

Urban growth and the expansion of cities brought about an increased need for urban transportation. At the beginning of the period most cities were fairly compact, and the built-up portions were negotiated easily by foot. In New York, for example, none of the heavily settled areas were more than a mile and three-quarters from City Hall. But particularly during the 1830s and '40s, population moved rapidly northward, and by 1860 the city was fairly well settled to at least Forty-second Street, which meant that substantially populated areas were now between three and four miles from City Hall. While Boston did not expand very much during these years, its population moved outward into adjacent towns. Philadelphia was relatively small in area, until its boundaries were expanded in 1854 to include the entire county of Philadelphia. Clearly, this physical growth created a need for improved urban transportation; but at the same time, improvements in transportation made continued growth possible.

City governments did not provide transportation facilities. The various modes of transportation were owned by individuals and private companies. Basically, three types of urban transportation were available: cabs, omnibuses, and street railways. In each case, motive power was supplied by horses. Travel by cab was the most private and the most expensive, so expensive that it essentially was restricted to the very wealthy. From about 1830 through the 1850s the most popular means of urban transportation was the omnibus. The omnibus typically was drawn by two horses and carried perhaps a dozen passengers on seats along both sides of the interior or standing in the center aisle. It operated over a fixed route on city streets, and picked up and dropped off passengers at frequent intervals. The passenger entered through a door in the rear. When arriving at his or her destination, the passenger pulled on a leather strap that ran along near the roof of the omnibus. This signaled the driver, who sat up on the outside of the vehicle, that a passenger wanted to leave. The passenger then gave the driver the fare through a hole in the roof, and the driver released the door so the passenger could leave. All passengers paid the same fare no matter how far they traveled. Most large American cities had omnibus lines prior to 1860. The largest and busiest lines were in New York, Philadelphia, and Boston. Some other cities in which omnibus lines were established were Baltimore, Washington, Pittsburgh, Detroit, and Chicago. Although omnibuses were quite numerous on the streets of the busiest cities, they were inadequate for the task of moving the burgeoning populations.

In the 1830s the idea of urban railways was proposed, and privately incorporated, horse-drawn street railway systems were developed. Although set back by the Panic of 1837, by the 1850s they were becoming fairly common. The great era of building street railways took place between 1852 and 1860. The first cars resembled omnibuses, but ran on rails in the city streets. By the late 1850s the cars were much larger, and usually were drawn by two horses. They seated approximately forty passengers, but they might hold as many as sixty or sixty-five. There also were some larger and heavier cars, like those commonly used on steam railroads, that needed as many as four or six horses to move them through the streets. New York, Brooklyn, Philadelphia, and Boston were very active in the establishment of street railway lines, but before the end of the 1850s street railways were being put into operation in other large American cities. In 1859 and 1860 they were constructed in Baltimore, Chicago, Cincinnati, Pittsburgh, and St. Louis. Streetcars had many advantages over omnibuses. They were smoother, quieter, less prone to accidents, faster, and carried more passengers. They also were cheaper to operate, since a horse could pull a greater load over rails. To some extent, the streetcar helped spread the city outward. As lines came to be extended to the nearby suburbs, many city dwellers were able to escape from the crowded living conditions of the central city. However, for the most part, unskilled workers were less able to take advantage of this opportunity than those who received higher incomes. Although a round-trip typically cost only 10 cents, that was a considerable sum to a worker earning no more than $2.00 a day. Moreover, the streetcars were not fast enough for workers who spent ten or more hours a day on the job. So even the streetcars did little to relieve population density in the slums of America's major cities.

Municipal Government. To understand the development of municipal government during the years between 1820 and 1860, it is first necessary to look at some changes that occurred as a result of the American Revolution and in the years that followed. Since cities existed by virtue of charters granted under British authority, during and after the Revolution it was common for new charters to be issued by the new states. In doing so, the state legislatures established what would become a tradition of state involvement in city affairs. Because cities were seen to owe their existence to state legislatures, a principle was established that city charters were state laws that could be amended by the legislatures. Furthermore, cities could exercise only those powers enumerated in the charters. That meant that if the cities wanted to undertake new functions, they would have to obtain the consent of the state legislatures, which were dominated by rural interests.

An important trend to be noted was that the electorate in cities was being broadened, and by the 1850s the right to vote in city elections was fairly widely extended to all adult white males; and many cities extended the vote to newcomers who indicated that they would become citizens. Another important trend had to do with the organization of municipal governments. In the early years of the nineteenth century most cities had a legislative body known as the city council, common council, board of aldermen, or similar designations. Most cities also had a mayor. At first the mayor was an appointed official of the state government, but gradually the mayor came to be elected by the common council. The mayor would work with the council in an executive capacity, but would have very little power on his own. The administrative functions of the city would be performed by the "mayor-in-council." As early as the 1820s, some mayors began to be popularly elected, and by the 1850s most mayors were chosen in popular elections. As that took place, mayors gradually were separated from the councils and no longer presided over their meetings. In time, mayors gained veto power over acts of the councils, and those vetoes required a two-thirds council vote to be overridden. Still, mayors were not completely trusted, so very few cities granted them appointing powers. Frequent elections and rotation in office were seen as ways to ensure that officials were responsible to the people, and so most mayors and council members were elected annually. Mayors usually only held their offices for one or two terms, since being mayor was not considered a stepping-stone to higher political office, but rather a duty to be undertaken by a respected businessman. The original unicameral councils also tended to become bicameral, and become primarily concerned with legislation, rather than administration. Some of those administrative functions were taken over by the mayor, but most of them went to independently elected heads of administrative departments. Gradually, voters were being called upon to elect many administrators and commission members, and because they were elected they became autonomous. The result of this was that voters were called upon to elect an increasing number of city officials, and elections became very confusing. So, too, did the operation of city governments. The administration of the city was divided among a large number of unrelated agencies, and no attempt was made at coordination. This fragmentation of power made it impossible to fix responsibility, and corruption became much easier to achieve.

CHAPTER 4

BECOMING AN URBAN NATION: 1860–1920

Even though the years from 1820–1860 were a time of tremendous urban growth in the United States, in 1860 the overwhelming majority of Americans lived in rural areas. Over the course of the next sixty years that was to change. The census of 1920 revealed that, for the first time, most Americans were living in areas the census classified as urban. And while many of these people lived in small and medium-sized cities, most urban dwellers inhabited cities of substantial size. In 1860 the largest cities numbered their populations in the hundreds of thousands; in 1920 there were three with populations of well over a million (New York, Chicago, Philadelphia), and a fourth city (Detroit) was approaching the one million mark. This was an era of great economic expansion for the United States, and its cities not only profited from it, they were instrumental in bringing it about.

The Economic Basis of Urban Growth. Throughout these years, commerce continued to be a very important factor in the urban economy. The railroad was the most important highway of commerce, and the expansion of the railroads not only contributed to the prosperity of the older cities, it also was essential to the establishment and growth of new cities.

In the East, railroading was characterized by consolidation. The gauge of railroad tracks was standardized, single-tracked lines became double tracked, and many formerly unconnected lines were now linked. This era saw the formation of major railroad lines, such as the New York Central, the Pennsylvania, and the Baltimore and Ohio. One result of this was to broaden the commercial contacts of the cities along their routes. At the same time, however, it resulted in commercial activity becoming centered in a few large cities. Moreover, as the railroad companies became larger and more powerful, they were able to dictate terms to cities; and this was true in all regions of the country. Although the fight to regulate railroads seemed to originate with farm groups, at least in the East, the call for regulation emanated from cities. City merchants and some other business leaders frequently opposed the great monopolistic railroads. Even New York could be ignored, to some extent, by railroad

59

interests. By 1869 Commodore Vanderbilt had gained complete control
of the New York Central and Hudson River Railroad, and he extended
the line until it reached Chicago and Toronto. This certainly was advantageous to the public, since freight service was improved and travel became more convenient; but it also meant that the railroad did not have
to cater to the commercial interests of cities along its route—even those
of New York. J. Edgar Thomson developed the Pennsylvania Railroad
into an extensive system by extending it west of Pittsburgh to Chicago
and St. Louis; but he also ran a line from Philadelphia to New York,
which, in effect, turned Philadelphia into a way station. Baltimore fared
somewhat better. Under the leadership of John W. Garrett, the Baltimore and Ohio Railroad also tried to run service into New York, but to
do so he would have had to run track through Pennsylvania, and in that
he was blocked. Instead, Garrett turned his attention to building up the
port of Baltimore.

In the South, the old port cities had suffered considerable harm as a
result of the Civil War, but in the postwar years new cities grew up as
rail centers. These rail centers were mainly interior cities such as Atlanta, Nashville, Louisville, Memphis, Dallas, and Birmingham. Atlanta was growing as a rail center as early as the 1850s, but the Civil
War resulted in the destruction of Atlanta's railroads. Still, recovery after the war was rapid, and it was railroad activity more than anything
else that contributed to Atlanta's growth. In 1860, the population of Atlanta was only 9,554, but in 1920 it was nearly 201,000. Louisville had
been an important commercial city serving the entire South before the
Civil War, and it had engaged in a rivalry with Cincinnati over control
of river trade and railroad expansion. After the war, Louisville worked
to regain and expand its commercial position, and it continued its rivalry with Cincinnati. Louisville was in a good position to do this. The
city's principal railroad, the Louisville and Nashville, had been an important military supply route, so it emerged from the war in excellent
condition. Further, the city was well located for the Ohio River trade,
and its merchants made much of he idea that they were "southern,"
while those in rival Cincinnati were "northern." Favorable legislation
was secured through vigorous lobbying in the Kentucky legislature, and
millions of dollars were allocated to improving transportation facilities.
Birmingham developed somewhat later than these other cities. In 1860
its population was only 3,086, but by 1920 it was nearly 179,000. While
industry was the major cause of Birmingham's growth, it was rail con-

nections that made it possible for industry to develop there. Further-more, it was the railroad interests that provided some of the early capital for Birmingham's iron mills.

But it was in the West that the greatest railroad activity took place with the building of the transcontinental lines. The railroad was essential to the growth of western cities, and the major west coast cities were those that had rail links to the East by way of the transcontinental lines. San Francisco, of course, developed before there were transcontinental rail lines. It originally had some importance because of trade and location, and it certainly received a tremendous boost from the gold rush. But the most permanent growth resulted from its being the western terminus of the first transcontinental railroad. In 1860 its population was 56,802. By 1870, though, it achieved a place among the ten largest cities in the United States, with a population of 150,000 (*See Document No. 14.*), and by 1920 it had reached 507,000. Los Angeles presents an excellent example of a city taking bold action to determine its future. The Southern Pacific Railroad originally planned to build its terminal at San Bernardino, but it indicated a willingness to establish it in Los Angeles instead, if that city would provide a subsidy of $600,000, a free right of way, and sixty acres in the center of the city for a depot. This small city of only seven thousand inhabitants agreed to these terms, and the Southern Pacific came to Los Angeles. A few years later, a second railroad, the Santa Fe, came to the city. This resulted in a real estate boom and a railroad rate war, in which transcontinental fares were reduced to as low as $40. During these years and those that followed, Los Angeles grew rapidly in population. By 1890 it had increased to about 50,000, and by 1920 to about 577,000. The city of Tacoma owed its existence to the site being chosen for the western terminus of the Northern Pacific Railroad in 1873, but its growth was never as great as its boosters had predicted. To a great extent this was due to the energy and persistence of the citizens of Seattle, who had lost out to Tacoma in the bid to become the Northern Pacific Railroad's terminus. Realizing the importance of a transcontinental connection, and unable to get anywhere with the Northern Pacific, Seattle businessmen decided to build a railroad to link up with the Canadian Pacific. Afraid of the competition, the Northern Pacific bought out that line, and Seattle was then linked into the Northern Pacific system. Soon, that branch line was carrying more freight than was the main line into Tacoma. Meanwhile, the ambitious citizens of Seattle had persuaded James J. Hill to make their city the western terminus of the Great Northern Railroad, which began operating trains out of Seattle in 1893. Seattle's rail connections combined with its fine harbor on Puget Sound, put that city in an excellent position to capitalize on the 1897 discovery of gold in the Klondike. Seattle became the leading city in the Pacific Northwest. In 1870 its population had only been slightly more than a thousand, but it reached forty-three thousand in 1890. Growth was now very rapid, and by 1920 the population of Seattle was approximately 315,000.

Several western inland cities also owed their major growth to the railroad. One of these was Omaha, which was founded in 1854 and had a population of 1,883 in 1860. Its first big break came in 1864 when it was designated as the eastern terminus of the projected Union Pacific Railroad. This brought in workers, and business boomed. Aided by its railroad connection, Omaha became a major meat-packing city, and by 1890 its population was more than 140,000. This increased to 381,000 by 1920. The small cow town of Kansas City built the first bridge over the Missouri River in 1869, which enabled it to gain a rail connection to Chicago. It soon had connections with St. Louis and points farther west by way of the Kansas Pacific Railroad. Before long, as a result of vigorous activity, Kansas City was at the hub of ten rail lines. It became a major meat-packing city and the leading trade center for the prairie region, and its population grew from 4,418 in 1840, to 324,000 by 1920. Denver was founded as a result of the Pike's Peak gold rush of 1859, and it prospered as a mining town in the early years. When the first transcontinental railroad was being built the citizens of Denver tried to convince the railroad to come into their city, but the Union Pacific bypassed Denver. Instead, it passed through Cheyenne, Wyoming, which was 110 miles north. If the railroad would not come to Denver, Denver went to the railroad, building a spur line to Cheyenne. The same year that line was completed (1870), the Kansas Pacific reached Denver. These rail connections were instrumental in Denver's population growing from 4,759 in 1870, to nearly 36,000 ten years later. In 1871 work began on the Denver and Rio Grande Railroad to tap the mineral deposits of the Southwest. Soon, farmers and cattle raisers moved into the region, and Denver became the leading city in the high plains and the Rocky Mountain region. By 1890 its population was 107,000, and by 1910 it was 213,000. Capitalizing on a reputedly healthy climate and the attractions of the mountain country, Denver turned to tourism as an industry, which was greatly expanded with the increasing popularity of the automobile. (*See Document No. 15.*) But rail connections alone did not ensure great growth for a city; other factors also were important. Particularly, a city had to have a product to ship. Cheyenne provides a good example of this point. That city was established by a land agent of the Union Pacific Railroad, and in 1867 in had only one house. But as the tracks approached a boom began, and Cheyenne had at least six thousand inhabitants by 1868, and contained at least three thousand houses. Land prices skyrocketed and business boomed. The railroad moved westward, though, and much of the business went with it. The region, much of which is semi-arid or mountainous, remained largely undeveloped, and Cheyenne never became a significant urban center.

As important as commerce was to urban growth, an even more dramatic impact came from the great progress being made in the development of manufacturing industries in the United States during this period. There was a symbiotic relationship between the two: In part, urban development made industrial progress possible, and in part, industrialization spurred urban growth. The transportation networks made possible the movement of raw materials and manufactured goods, and surplus capital from commerce helped establish and expand manufacturing enterprises. The growing city populations also supplied the labor force, as well as ready markets for the products of industry. Older commercial cities often gained new wealth and prominence by turning to manufacturing, while new cities were emerging as industrial centers. Technology played an important role, not only through the improvement of production methods, but also through the introduction of new products. Significantly, the process of building cities and their infrastructures constituted one of the nation's biggest industries.

In 1860 New York was in first place among American cities when ranked according to value of manufactured products, and it also was the nation's leading manufacturing city in 1910. Unlike most other industrial centers, New York did not have a few dominant companies producing products in huge factories. Instead, that city had a diversity of industries and many small factories. For example, in 1900 New York contained nearly forty thousand manufacturing concerns that produced one-tenth of the nation's factory output. The largest of those industries was involved in the production of clothing. The garment industry began there in the mid-nineteenth century, and it was spurred on by government contracts during the Civil War. The most enterprising businessmen during the early years were German Jews, but after a while East European Jews came to dominate. A contract system developed, under which the contractor would employ fellow countrymen to work for him in a loft or in his own apartment. Because large machinery was not needed for this work—sewing machines were portable and were operated by foot power—the work could be done in small units. Other New York industries of importance were printing and publishing, machine and foundry products, foods, and chemicals. New York's excellent transportation facilities, cheap immigrant labor, and the availability of capital were the major reasons for its industrial development. Yet commerce still was the mainstay of New York's economy. In 1900, New York's port accounted for 37 percent of exports from the United States and 67 percent of imports. This commercial and industrial activity was reflected in the city's population growth. In 1860 the combined population of New York and Brooklyn was 1,093,000; in 1920 there were 4,767,000 people living in New York (which now included Brooklyn).

By 1910 Chicago was the second-ranked manufacturing city in the United States; it had been only sixteenth in 1860. Its leading industry was meat packing. Very significant to the development of that enterprise was the 1865 opening of the Union Stockyards, four miles southwest of the city. That huge operation covered nearly a square mile, and it contained not only pens for the animals, but also hotels, restaurants, and an exchange. The yards were served by nine railroads, and a small canal connected it with the river. The introduction of refrigerator cars in 1869 also was very important to this industry. Chicago remained the nation's leading meat-packing city until the 1950s. But meat packing was only one of Chicago's important industries. That city ranked second only to New York in printing and publishing, and it was second only to New York in the men's clothing industry. The manufacture of agricultural implements was another of Chicago's important industries. As early as 1870, the huge McCormick plant was one of the city's principal employers. The steel industry, too, was becoming increasingly significant, and by 1910 Chicago surpassed Pittsburgh in steel output. All of this industrial growth resulted from Chicago being at the center of rail and lake transportation, from its having a vast hinterland that provided raw materials, and from its large population that provided a labor pool. (*See Document No. 16.*) And that population grew at a phenomenal rate— from 112,000 in 1860, to 2,700,000 in 1920.

By 1880 Detroit had become a manufacturing city of some importance, but the industry most associated with it had yet to emerge. In the 1890s some Detroit citizens, like those in several other cities, were experimenting with automobiles. By 1910, though, Detroit led the nation in automobile production. Why this happened is something of a mystery, except for the fact that some of the most innovative pioneers in the industry happened to reside in Detroit. The manufacturers of automobiles in Detroit borrowed ideas from other industries, such as interchangeable parts and assembly-line production, and adapted them to this new industry. One of the most important of these men was Ransom E. Olds, the first automobile entrepreneur to apply precision manufacturing and mass production. The components of his vehicles were made by other manufacturers, and then were assembled in his factory. Perhaps even more important than Olds, was Henry Ford, whose idea it was to produce automobiles that could be afforded by farmers and working-class Americans. (*See Document No. 17.*) The industry grew rapidly, and before the end of the period the General Motors Corporation had been organized, and its main headquarters was located in Detroit. The automobile industry contributed greatly to Detroit's population increase. The number of residents in Detroit in 1860 was forty-six thousand. The early years of the industry's development brought that number to 286,000 by 1900; but by 1920, with the rapidly increasing popularity of the automobile, the population of Detroit soared to 994,000.

Surely no city in the United States has been more identified with industrial activity than Pittsburgh, and the industry most linked to Pittsburgh has been iron and steel. A local supply of bituminous coal and ready access to iron ore deposits of the West were significant in Pittsburgh becoming the major producer of iron and steel. Andrew Carnegie was very important in the development of the steel industry. He began building his steel empire in the 1870s, and an important step was taken in 1883, when Carnegie and associates bought the Homestead Steel Works. Later, Carnegie sold out to the Morgan interests, who formed United States Steel in 1901. Although by far the largest, Carnegie steel interests were not the only ones in Pittsburgh; there were several other important producers, such as Jones and Laughlin. The glass industry was one of the oldest manufacturing activities in Pittsburgh. As early as 1870, half the nation's output of glass was produced there. (*See Document No. 18.*) An important development came in 1895 with the formation of the giant Pittsburgh Plate Glass Company. Beginning in the early 1870s, several other manufacturing enterprises were established by George Westinghouse, who was a very important innovator. Among his contributions to the advance of technology were the air brake, a railroad signal system, and the use of alternating current for electric power transmission. In 1886 the Westinghouse Electric Company was formed in Pittsburgh. Still another significant Pittsburgh industry began in the 1870s, when Henry John Heinz started his food processing company. And by the late 1880s, the aluminum industry began in Pittsburgh. All of these developments led to substantial population growth. While Pittsburgh was already a good-sized city in 1860, with seventy-eight thousand inhabitants, by 1920 more than 588,000 people lived there.

Milwaukee was another rapidly growing industrial city. Between 1870 and 1910 the annual value of manufactured products increased more than tenfold in Milwaukee. The most successful of Milwaukee's enterprises was the brewing industry. The output of the city's brewers was twenty-six times greater in 1910 than it had been in 1871. One of the reasons for this was the high-powered advertising techniques employed by Milwaukee breweries, especially Pabst and Schlitz, in their attempt to capture urban markets. Other industries, too, contributed substantially to the city's economy. Milwaukee was an important center for meat packing and tanning and iron and steel production. The city also contained many foundries and machine shops. The industrialization of Milwaukee was accompanied by a dramatic population increase; there were more than ten times as many people living in Milwaukee in 1920 (457,000) than there were in 1860 (45,000).

There are a good number of other cities that might be cited as examples of the contribution of manufacturing to urban growth, but perhaps one more illustration will suffice, and that is of a city considerably smaller than those already discussed. Schenectady, New York, is an example of a city rising to importance because of new technology. In 1886 Thomas Edison was interested in moving the Edison Machine Works to Schenectady. A representative of the company discovered two empty factory buildings there that he considered suitable. Edison made an offer, but the owners set a price that was $7,500 more than he was willing to pay. Realizing the importance of this industry to the city, a group of local civic leaders raised the additional money from among the city's businessmen. In the 1890s the General Electric Corporation was formed and took over the Edison plant in Schenectady. In 1894 General Electric chose Schenectady as its main headquarters, and in 1900 established its research laboratory there. Earlier, the American Locomotive Company had been established in Schenectady. And so, by 1900 local boosters proudly proclaimed as the city's motto: "Schenectady Lights and Hauls the World." In 1880, before the Edison factory was established there, the city's population was only fourteen thousand; by 1920 it was ninety-six thousand.

Financing for all this industrial expansion increasingly was coming from banks in major cities. Although New York banks were always important, by the 1860s they were becoming especially dominant. Banks in Philadelphia and Boston also continued to be nationally significant, and banks in other large cities were of regional importance. Large-scale industrial growth required the issuing of stocks and bonds, and so the role of security and commodity exchanges expanded. The oldest of these was the New York Stock Exchange, which had been founded in 1817. By the 1860s it was the pre-eminent exchange in America, but with the increasing importance of industrial securities by the 1880s, it became even more significant. Other major cities, such as Chicago, San Francisco, and Memphis, had security and commodity exchanges that served regional needs. The growth of banking and investment made the urban sector even more influential in the development of the American economy, but New York was the prime beneficiary of this industry's expansion. Before the period was over, a small group of New York investment bankers had come to control much of the railroad and industrial activity of the United States. New York was not only the nation's leading center for commerce and industry, it also was the financial center of the country.

The People of the City. The substantial growth in the urban population was attributable to several sources. The most obvious source would be natural increase, that is, the surplus of births over deaths. This factor, though, cannot account for the tremendous increase in the urban population during these years. In fact, by 1900 there was considerable alarm over declining birth rates. While that was true, improvements in sanitation and other health measurers resulted in a considerable surplus of births over deaths, and that trend was continuing. Less obvious, and more difficult to quantify, was the increase in urban population that came about through the process of annexation. The cities of America were expanding physically, and in doing so they took over populated areas that had been outside the city limits. Many of the residents of those

areas welcomed annexation, which would bring them many public services that the cities were instituting. The result, though, was that many
people became urban dwellers without ever moving to the city.

Much more significant was the migration from country to city, which
was the major source of urban population until at least 1900. This was
true not only for the United States, but also throughout Europe. Agriculture in Europe was becoming an unprofitable means of earning a living, and so many agricultural laborers were moving to cities. Although
absolute declines in European rural populations were not common, relative declines were quite pronounced. Because of the movement of European agricultural workers to the cities in Europe, even the movement of
European immigrants to the United States may be looked at as a migration from country to city. In the United States a statistical analysis con-
firms that the principal source of urban growth was from rural areas.
Between 1860 and 1900 the cities of America grew more that twice as
fast as the total population, and while farm population was half again as
large, the urban population was four times what it had been. Furthermore, many rural townships were actually declining in population, especially in New England. One way to demonstrate that immigration
could not have been the major source of the tremendous increase in urban populations would be to subtract all the immigrants who came to
the United States between 1860 and 1900 from the non-farm population of 1900. This would be an exaggerated figure, since we know that
many immigrants did take up farming. Nonetheless, the remaining figure would still show the urban population increasing at twice the rate
of the non-urban population.

Why were rural dwellers flocking to the cities in such great numbers?
One reason was the psychological lure of the city. Farm life was isolated
and lonely. Especially in the less developed areas of the Middle West,
farms were widely separated, partly as a result of the pattern of settlement established by the Homestead Act. Even in the more settled areas,
though, neighbors were fairly far away. Moreover, communications were
poor; there was no rural mail delivery, and there were no telephones. In
contrast to this, the city offered daily social contact. Furthermore, farm
work was hard and monotonous, and opportunities for amusement to
relieve the tedium of work were few. What amusements there were
seemed insignificant when compared with the entertainment facilities
available in the city. By and large, it was only in the cities, where large

populations made it profitable, that professional entertainment, of whatever form, could flourish.

Another reason why many country people migrated to the city was the opportunity to make a living. Farm life was not as economically attractive as it had once been. For one thing, the cost of farms and farming was increasing. More land and more expensive equipment were necessary for farming to be profitable. To purchase land and equipment more capital was needed, and that resulted in farmers being indebted to banks. Eastern farmers were particularly disadvantaged, since western farmers typically had more land that was more fertile. On the other hand, farmers were constantly hearing about the greater wealth that was to be found in the cities. The tradition of the farm in the late-nineteenth century became a tradition of failure, and in this age of increasing urban influence, the "sturdy yeoman" of earlier years had now become the "hayseed."

Contemporaries were well aware of this farm to city movement (*See Document No. 19.*), and not all looked upon it with favor. A considerable effort was made to convince the farmer to remain on the farm. This effort took the form of books, magazine and newspaper articles, speeches, and so forth. Most tried to portray the city as a corrupt, evil place, as contrasted to the farm, which was the embodiment of American virtues. Country boys and girls were advised to remain in their rural homes, for residency in the city surely would lead to loss of virtue, if not worse. Some titles of popular books were: W. F. Howe and A. H. Hummel, *Danger: A True History of a Great City's Wiles and Temptations*; E. W. Martin, *The Secrets of the Great City*; Rev. Henry Morgan, *Boston Inside Out! Sins of a Great City!* (*See Document No. 20.*) By and large, this propaganda did not achieve its desired objectives, and perhaps the loss of farm youth to the cities was not as disastrous as many rural spokesmen believed. Rural areas did continue to grow for the most part, and productivity increased. Surplus farm labor was moving to the cities, which reduced unemployment in rural areas. Moreover, the large urban populations became important as consumers of the increased output of the farms.

Just as white Americans were moving to the cities, so too were black Americans. By 1890 nearly 20 percent of the black population of the United States was urban, and this grew to 34 percent by 1920. After the Civil War there was a sizable movement of former slaves into southern cities. Former slaves felt insecure in the rural South, and they knew even before the war that conditions in the cities were better than in the rural regions. Now, they would demonstrate their freedom by seeking the advantages offered by the city. At first, these new urban dwellers seemed to be making progress in their struggle to gain the rights of citizens; but the white response was hostile. Southern whites feared this large influx of blacks, which they saw as a threat to "white civilization." They saw to it that African Americans were relegated to the least desirable occupations, and that they were segregated in all aspects of life. That segregation did not result in the formation of large black ghettos at this time. Instead, blacks lived in small, disconnected segregated slum communities on the outskirts of the cities, where they were surrounded by lower-class whites. Because of this residential pattern and their limited resources, southern black urban dwellers were not in a position to do much about segregation and discrimination.

The migration of blacks to the North had been small until 1890, but it increased during the next decade, and it had its greatest impact during World War I. It has been estimated that eighty-eight thousand blacks left the South between 1880 and 1890. By 1910–1920 the net migration of blacks from the South was approximately 450,000. Most of these people settled in the cities, so that by 1890 60 percent of African Americans in the North and West were urban dwellers. That migration was primarily to the large cities. The principal reasons for this migration to northern cities appear to have been economic, although social disabilities in the South clearly played a role. Also, just as rural whites were attracted by the lure of the city, so too were rural blacks.

Black residents of northern cities faced similar disabilities as those who lived in southern cities. Northern attitudes towards blacks certainly were made clear early in the period with the New York Draft Riots of 1863. These riots began on July 13, 1863, and they lasted for four days. This was the worst civil disorder in United States history. The rioters were people at the bottom of the socioeconomic order, primarily Irish immigrants, and they were striking out against government control. To a great extent, though, their frustrations were taken out on New York's black residents, a number of whom were lynched and burned, and one of the buildings burned was the Colored Orphan Asylum. In the years that followed, black residents of northern cities, like those of southern cities, were only able to find employment in jobs that were considered the least desirable. They also had to contend with residential segregation. As the cities expanded outward, African Americans and other poor people were pushed inward to the center, and the previously dispersed black neighborhoods began to merge and form inner-city ghettos. Because choice of residence was restricted, these areas became overcrowded. Any attempts to move from the ghettos were opposed by lower- and middle-class whites. Houses were bombed, crosses were burned, racial covenants were added to mortgages and deeds, and at times riots erupted, such as the notorious Chicago riot of 1919. While the ghettos offered African Americans the advantage of having their own communities, and thus the ability to exercise some independence, they were still economically and politically dominated by whites.

The other important element of the urban population, of course, was the foreign born. From 1860 into the 1880s, more than ten million immigrants came to the United States. Most of them came from Germany, Ireland, England, Scotland, and Scandinavia. Many of the immigrants from the British Isles went to the cities of America. British immigrants came in great numbers until the 1880s, when migrants from Britain began to move into portions of the British Empire.

In the years following the Civil War, many Americans were more accepting of the Irish than they had been earlier; after all, the Irish had fought and died for the Union, and had thus demonstrated their patriotism. Still, the Irish continued to be stereotyped as perhaps likeable, but nonetheless ignorant, boisterous, and frequently imbibing too much whiskey. In cartoons they were shown as crude and ignorant and bearing a resemblance to monkeys. Certainly, the Irish were not considered acceptable in "proper society." There was a concern, too, that the Irish would never be assimilated into the mainstream of American life, since they continued to be ardent Irish nationalists and to commemorate old-country events, such as St. Patrick's Day. There also was concern over the increasing political power of the Irish on the local level, and American Protestants feared the growth of Catholicism. Often, the Irish ended up in conflict with other foreign-born groups. Those groups who arrived after the Irish discovered that the Irish were in control of most things that mattered to them—jobs, politics, and, to the large number of immigrants who were Catholic, the church. Before the Irish arrived in the United States, the Catholic Church was small in numbers and influence; but the great influx of Irish changed that, and soon the Catholic Church in America was dominated by Irish clergy. The Irish priests often were contemptuous of the newer immigrants, whose religious customs were different from theirs. On the other hand, Italians and Poles would rather attend their own churches, and while national churches officially were prohibited in the United States by Rome, in practice they often existed.

The German migration to the United States during this period was very large, having reached an annual migration of thirty thousand by the late 1870s. It increased to 110,000 in 1880, and it reached a high point of 250,000 in 1882. The main reasons for this migration are to be found in economic changes resulting from the shift in Germany to an industrial society, high taxes, and the requirement of compulsory military training. By the 1890s, though, the migration declined, reflecting Germany's great advances as an industrial nation, growing prosperity, and the successful adoption of progressive social legislation. The Germans who came to the United States after 1870 were a somewhat different group than those who had migrated earlier. This latter group contained fewer peasants and more industrial workers and artisans, and the intellectual and cultural leadership of the earlier group was less apparent. Still, these migrants frequently had some education and were not usually destitute when they arrived in the United States. They also were less critical of the German government, and community leaders tried to preserve the German language and culture in the United States. Some Germans occupied leadership positions in socialist organizations in America, and a few radicals became involved in the anarchist movement; but most Germans were much more interested in social gatherings and in earning a living than they were in radical politics.

Between the 1880s and 1914 more than fifteen million immigrants arrived in the United States. They came mainly from Italy, Greece, Romania, Austria-Hungary, and Russia, and there also were some from the Middle East and the Far East. Even more than their predecessors, these immigrants tended to concentrate in the cities. A result of this concentration was that contemporaries frequently were convinced that there were more foreign-born in America than ever before. (*See Document No. 21.*) Although this clearly was true of actual numbers, the proportion was not very much greater. In 1860 the foreign-born constituted 13.2 percent of the population; by 1910 they accounted for 14.5 percent. However, the change in the character of immigration was quite pronounced. In the early 1880s, 87 percent of the immigrants arriving in the United States had come from northern and western Europe; in

1907, 81 percent came from southern and eastern Europe. An important reason for the increased immigration from those areas may be found in the development of transportation facilities to eastern and southern Europe.

In 1880 a little more than twelve thousand Italians entered the United States, but by 1900 the yearly minimum was a hundred thousand. The peak year came in 1907, when 285,731 Italians entered the United States. For a while, as many as fifteen thousand Italians were landing at Ellis Island in a single day. The earliest migrants were from northern Italy, but after 1900 the great majority were from southern Italy, especially from Calabria, the Abruzzi district, or Sicily. Economic factors were primary among the reasons for the Italian migration. Soil depletion, overpopulation, and high taxes pushed them out of Italy; the prospect of employment brought them to America. The majority of these immigrants arrived at a time when workers were needed in the United States; and the wages, two to five times higher than in Italy, looked good. Low rates for an ocean crossing contributed to this migration; steerage passenger rates from Naples to New York were $15 in 1880 and $28 in 1900.

Most of the Italian migrants to the United States had been farmers in Italy, but in America they usually settled in the cities. However, it is a mistake to make too much of this, because there was a great difference between American farmers and Italian farmers. While American farmers lived isolated on their farms, Italian peasant farmers lived in agricultural communities that sometimes contained as many as twenty thousand people. Each morning the Italian farmer left the community to work in the fields, and each evening he returned. Moreover, these agricultural workers often possessed some skills other than farming, and on occasion worked at jobs outside the rural community. There were a variety of reasons why they preferred living in cities in the United States. Certainly, being with other Italians was important, but the availability of employment at wages above those received by agricultural workers also was important. Another reason may be found in the pattern of migration. Approximately two-thirds of the Italians who came to the United States during this period were men. They usually came alone, or with a brother, son, or other male of working age. Many of them worked in the United States to save enough money to bring over the rest of the family; but there were many who went to the United States, worked for a while, and then returned to Italy. Migrants such as these were known as "birds of passage," and many made the ocean crossings several times. For those who worked to bring their families over, and for those who worked with the intention of going back to Italy, the city was a good location.

Many of these new immigrants from Italy secured their first jobs through a *padrone*, who was someone who spoke Italian and had contacts with prospective employers. Some of these *padroni* were unscrupulous, promising good jobs that turned out to be a sham, advancing funds at high interest rates, and charging fees that left immigrants with large debts. But not all were, and they did provide a service in helping the immigrants get jobs. Most of those jobs involved heavy labor, and many Italians worked as construction workers and day laborers, but about 10 percent of Italian men worked in skilled trades. A substantial number of Italian women and children found employment in factories, especially in the garment trade, where they worked under sweatshop conditions. In time, some moved into the food supply area, especially catering to the desire of Italian communities for their traditional foods.

In many of the cities in which they settled, Italians soon formed "Little Italys." To outside observers these appeared to be homogeneous ethnic enclaves, but they were not seen that way by their residents. Instead, they were divided into areas representing the parts of Italy from which their occupants had migrated, and so portions might be inhabited primarily by Sicilians, Genoese, Calabrians, and so forth. The residents of each section tried to preserve their own ethnic roots, and they often did not trust those who came from other parts of Italy. There also was some suspicion of outsiders, particularly the Irish. Religion was one area of conflict with the Irish, who, as has been noted earlier, dominated the Catholic Church in America. This conflict with the Irish also carried over into politics. While the Irish and most other immigrant groups tended to be loyal to the Democratic Party, the Italians were more likely to support the Republican Party.

The Greeks were another group migrating to the United States from southern Europe, although in comparison to other European nations the numbers were small. This was primarily a male migration; in fact, between 1899 and 1910 men comprised 95 percent of Greek immigrants. Clearly, the purpose of this migration was to earn money and then return to Greece, so even more than among the Italians these people would be characterized as "birds of passage." In Greece most had been farmers, but they usually chose to live in the cities of the United States, which offered them jobs and a social life. Farming in Greece was very different from in the United States, and, like the Italians, Greek farmers were used to a communal existence. The earliest Greeks to settle in American cities tended to work at petty street trades. They lived a very frugal existence so they could save money to send to relatives back in Greece. Those relatives often would lend that money out at high interest rates. Beginning in the 1890s significant numbers of Greeks were finding employment in factories, and others found jobs in railroad construction. Still others worked in a variety of unskilled trades, and a smaller number in skilled occupations. A few had managed to own and manage their own shops. And, like the Italians, some Greeks developed a *padrone* system, which was most common in the shoe-shining business.

Greek immigrants wanted to preserve Greek cultural, religious, and social traditions within their American communities, and they were fairly successful in doing this. Maintaining the Greek language was central to this effort, and schools were established to teach that language to the community's children. Greeks also were active in forming fraternal societies, which tended to represent Greek villages or parishes. This provincialism was quite pronounced among the Greeks, who preferred to work and socialize with compatriots from the same regions of Greece. Greek men also would have preferred to marry women from their provinces, and so they often would have to seek wives in Greece. However, given the overwhelming proportion of men among the Greeks in America, marriages to non-Greeks were more common than the communities would admit.

Among Slavic migrants to the United States, the Poles were the largest group, and they also were the third largest group in the history of American immigration. Still, it is not possible to be certain of just how many Poles did come to the United States, since Poland, as a modern nation, did not exist until after World War I; rather, Poland was divided into regions under Russian, German, and Austrian rule. As a result, immigration officials often listed Poles as citizens of other countries. The main migration of Poles into the United States did not begin until 1870, and during the next ten years thirty-five thousand Poles came to America. From then on, the migration grew significantly, with 236,000 arriving from 1880–90, and 875,000 from 1900–10. By 1920 there were three million people of Polish parentage in the United States. There were a variety of reasons for this heavy migration, but primary among them was the promise of greater economic opportunity in the United States.

This did not mean that conditions in Poland were so bad that potential migrants faced starvation; rather, migration was seen as a way of improving economic status or, in some cases, of at least maintaining it. Those who migrated were mostly landless peasants who had no possibility of acquiring land or of improving their economic situation. (*See Document No. 22.*) At first migration was seen as abandoning the community, but as the number of Poles in America grew, Polish communities in the United States seemed almost like an extension of those in Poland. Moreover, it often was insisted that the migration to America was only temporary, and a fair number of Poles were "birds of passage." Those who did remain in America, though, seem to have believed they had an obligation to return.

Among the Poles in the United States, approximately a third became farmers, but most became unskilled mine and factory workers, and they were most numerous in the northeastern quarter of the country, where heavy industry and mining were concentrated. Large numbers settled in eastern cities, like New York, but the most significant populations were in the lake cities and in other heavy-labor cities. By 1920 New York's Polish population was 250,000, but Chicago had the largest Polish community in the country—and the third largest in the world—with a population of about 350,000. Other substantial Polish populations were in Buffalo (80,000), Milwaukee (75,000), and Pittsburgh (200,000). In those and other cities, at least during the early years of settlement, there was a tendency for the Poles to cluster in groups representing different Polish provinces.

The major migration to the United States of East European Jews began in the 1870s, with forty thousand arriving during that decade. The movement became very much larger in the years that followed, with more than 200,000 arriving in the United States during the 1880s, and approximately 300,000 in the 1890s; and from 1900 to the outbreak of World War I about 1,500,000 more arrived. The total for the period exceeded two million, which represented more than a third of the Jews of eastern Europe. There were several major reasons for this migration. Both law and custom restricted these people in their occupations, and while some of them did manage to attain moderate financial success, large numbers lived in poverty. Opportunities for economic improvement were very limited, and they were becoming even more restricted. Then, beginning in the 1880s there were a series violent anti-Jewish outbreaks, known as pogroms, in which many were killed. Yet another significant reason for leaving was that young Jewish men were subject to involuntary military service for extended periods, which would make it impossible for them to practice their religion. Given these circumstances, then, it is not surprising that this was mainly a family migration, and unlike many other immigrants, few of these people had any intention of returning.

More than 90 percent of the East European Jews who migrated went to the United States, and while some of them settled in western cities, most took up residence in northeastern cities. New York was the usual port of entry to the United States, and the vast majority remained in that city. In New York they were able to maintain contact with coreligionists, as well as to take advantage of greater advancement and educational opportunities than would be found in rural areas or smaller cities. In New York, they resided primarily on the lower east side of Manhattan Island.

When first arriving in New York, many of the men found employment as peddlers. Others soon became involved in the food business to provide products that would conform to religious dietary laws. More Jews than members of other immigrant groups possessed industrial skills, and so they frequently found employment as hat and cap makers, furriers, tailors, bookbinders, watchmakers, cigarmakers, and tinsmiths, as well as in many other trades. In particular, many found employment in the clothing industry, and by 1914 they essentially had taken over that industry in New York. However, very few Jews were employed as day laborers. Women were an important part of the workforce, and they were especially numerous in the clothing trades.

As already noted, the East European Jews were crowded into New York's Lower East Side, and there they tended to cluster according to the regions of East Europe from which they had come. Although by 1900 this was the most densely inhabited portion of the city, they were inclined to remain there because this was where they found employment and where their social, cultural, and religious needs could be accommodated. After a while, though, they began to move out of the Lower East Side, establishing enclaves in neighborhoods in Brooklyn. As transportation improved, they moved into newly developing areas in upper Manhattan and the Bronx.

The Lower East Side had not only been the principal place of residence for East European Jews, it also was an important center of their culture. The most significant reason for this was that the language they spoke, Yiddish, was changing from a spoken vernacular to a written language. This process had begun in Europe, but it bore fruit in the United States. During these years there was a tremendous outpouring of publications in Yiddish. Under the editorship of Abraham Cahan, the Yiddish-language newspaper, *The Forward*, became a major force in the community. The Lower East Side also was the center for Yiddish theater, which was immensely popular. New York rapidly developed into the leading center for Jewish intellectual life.

CHAPTER 5

DEALING WITH THE PROBLEMS OF
URBAN GROWTH: 1860–1920

The expanding urban economy and the huge influx of people into America's cities presented many problems for which solutions needed to be found. The burgeoning urban populations, of all economic strata, required housing. It also was necessary to address the many social problems brought about by urban growth. Providing housing for people and structures for the needs of business required physical expansion of the city, and that expansion was upward as well as outward. The rapidly growing city also demanded an expansion of existing urban services and the imposition of new ones. All of this, of course, required administrative oversight, and so governments had to take on new functions.

Housing the People. There were two factors that were particularly important in determining the nature of housing for the urban masses, and these were the high cost of land and the gridiron plan typical of most cities. The high cost of land resulted in both the builder and the landowner wanting to make a maximum profit, and that meant realizing a maximum rental. The gridiron plan determined the size and shape of the lot. This meant a rectangular lot of 25 feet by 100 feet, as in New York, or 25 feet by 125 feet, as in Chicago. On this long, narrow lot the builder would erect a dwelling that would contain a maximum number of apartments. In New York this meant a five or six story building that occupied most of the lot, and because these structures were built with no intervening space between, there were many dark rooms. Apartments did not have toilets; there were either backyard privies or toilets in the basement. (*See Document No. 23.*) In other cities, such as Boston and Chicago, the "three-decker" became popular. These were four-story buildings, usually constructed of wood. The three upper stories had wooden balconies, either in the front or in the rear. Because the Chicago lot was deep, two or three of these might be erected on a single lot—one in the front, one in the rear on an alley, and sometimes one between these. Philadelphia and Baltimore continued to build row houses, and while endless streets of these were very monotonous, the congestion was less than in New York.

In the late 1870s a contest for the design of a better tenement was held in New York. The winner was a design for what was called the "dumbbell" tenement. The purpose of this design was to combine the most convenience for the tenant with the greatest profit for the owner. The owner faired far better than the tenant. These buildings usually were five or six stories high, with fourteen rooms on each floor, consisting of two four-room apartments and two three-room apartments. The hallway and stairs were in the center, and there were two toilets on each floor, which were located in the hallway. Ten of the fourteen rooms on each floor received light and air from an air shaft, and it was these air shafts that gave the building a cross-section that was the shape of a dumbbell. The air shaft, open only at the top, presented a fire and health hazard. Not only did the building occupy between 75 and 90 percent of the lot, the rooms were very small.

It was clear that the only way to ensure even barely adequate housing for the poor would be through legislation. The first law regulating tenement houses was passed in New York City in 1867, but it did not establish very high standards. Its provisions frequently were vague, and considerable discretion was given to the Board of Health. Nonetheless, the Tenement House Law of 1867 was very important symbolically, because it was a recognition of the acceptance in principle of the community's right to limit the freedom of the landlord and the builder. (*See Document No. 24.*) An improved code was passed in 1879, and it was amended in 1887, but the changes were not major and the code could not be enforced effectively. A greatly improved housing act was passed in 1901, which restricted the amount of the lot a tenement could occupy, required that each room have a window opening to the outside, required running water and a private toilet in each apartment, and prescribed a certain minimum of cubic feet of space for each occupant. The changes initiated by this law were so significant that tenements erected after it was passed were known as "new law," while earlier tenements were referred to as "old law." This law was widely copied. Boston's first tenement house law was passed in 1902, and the first meaningful legislation in Chicago was passed in 1905. During the first decade of the twentieth century housing codes were adopted in many cities.

If the houses of the poor amply illustrated their poverty, the houses of the rich displayed the wealth of their inhabitants. The use of a lavish urban dwelling to display the wealth of the millionaire really began in this era, and did not last much beyond it. New York, the largest and most important city in the nation, became the preferred location for the urban homes of the wealthiest Americans. Other cities, too, contained large mansions inhabited by their wealthiest citizens, but none of these houses could compare with the great stone palaces erected in New York. The first of these was the William K. Vanderbilt house on New York's Fifth Avenue. This was a great stone chateau that was designed by the noted architect, Richard Morris Hunt, and it was completed in 1881. It set the fashion for the residence of the urban millionaire. Richard M. Hunt and other leading architects designed many urban palaces in the years that followed.

Many other urban residents lived less lavishly in brownstone or brick houses. Brownstone was most popular in New York and Boston, but it commonly was used as far west as Chicago. By 1880 more than three quarters of the stone buildings in New York had brownstone fronts. Typically, the brownstone was used only for the front, with the sides and rear being built of brick. In some cities, especially in Philadelphia, brick remained the dominant construction material. In a few cities, but particularly in New York, urban houses were built side by side, without any open space between them.

In smaller cities and in new suburban areas, a housing style that became very popular was known as the "Queen Anne." Some of these may still be found in almost every community in America. The style dates to the 1876 Centennial Exhibition in Philadelphia, where the English Commission to the fair was housed in a group of buildings resembling English cottages, with half timbering and shingle work. Noone really knows why the picturesque style this inspired in America came to be called Queen Anne. Although these houses were built with many variations, there were some typical features. Usually, but not always, built of wood, they often were covered with shingles. Commonly, at one of the corners facing the street there was a round or octagonal tower. A wide veranda with spindled railings, a long, sharply pitched roof with peaked dormers, and several upstairs balconies recessed into the house were other typical features. One of the reasons why these houses had such widespread appeal was that they could be built in various sizes and degrees of luxury, and there seemed to be no limits to the variety of features that might be incorporated.

In 1870 a significant development in housing for urban dwellers was made in New York when the first modern apartment house was erected. The building was designed by Richard M. Hunt, and it took its inspiration from the apartment houses of Paris. It contained sixteen apartments, each of which had six rooms and a bath. At first, the early apartment houses, which were called "French flats," received considerable criticism, with many people seeing them as upscale tenements. But they were anything but tenements. Not only were the apartments spacious, but they also offered numerous services for their occupants, such as a kitchen that could prepare meals for the tenants, laundry services, and sometimes even a roof nursery. At first, apartment houses did not have elevator service, and so the apartments on the lower stories were more expensive than those on the upper stories. When elevator service was introduced, the rent scale was reversed, with apartments on the upper floors being more expensive, since they were quieter and less likely to be burglarized. Apartment-house living soon became very popular in New York, and by the end of 1875 the city contained 198 apartment houses, and by 1893 there were about seven hundred of them. Before very long, more apartment houses than single-family houses were being built in some major cities. There were several reasons why apartment houses were becoming increasingly popular. Servants were necessary to maintain large single-family houses, and it was becoming very difficult to obtain domestic servants. On the other hand, they were not necessary for apartment house living, since many services were provided by the owners of the buildings. The cost of building materials was rising and land was very expensive, and so few people could afford to buy single-family houses. And then, too, the size of the American family was decreasing, and so apartments could provide adequate living space. Even if people preferred to live in private homes, multiple-unit dwellings were more efficient, and the apartment house seemed to be the best solution to the problem of housing the rapidly growing urban populations.

Attempts at Social Reform. The huge influx of poor people into the cities by 1860 and the subsequent overcrowding, brought about social problems that were beyond the scope of existing charities. During the Civil War several new relief agencies had been formed that were to come under the aegis of the United States Sanitary Commission (the predecessor of the American Red Cross), and some efforts were made by this organization and some others to assist soldiers in the cities. But when the war was over there was a loss of interest in these activities. Still, there were some new charitable initiatives underway by the 1870s, such as the establishment of industrial schools for women and children and homes for working women.

While those with financial resources relied upon private physicians when they were ill, the poor had little choice but to resort to hospitals. It became clear, especially in the larger cities that more hospitals were needed, and some private citizens made bequests for that purpose. For the most part, though, people lacked confidence in hospitals, which were seen more as places where the ill went to die, rather than to recover. But after 1900, as medical knowledge rapidly improved, so too did public confidence in hospitals.

The public hygiene movement was more successful, with substantial advances having been made in the field of public health by the early twentieth century. Tuberculosis, a disease all too common in the crowded tenements, was of particular concern. To combat the spread of the disease, a successful campaign had been waged against spitting in public places; and because it was believed that fresh air would be therapeutic for those who had the disease, public and private sanitoriums were established outside the cities. Another important development in the public hygiene movement was the provision of public baths for tenement dwellers, who usually did not have adequate bathing facilities available in their homes.

The welfare of children was of increasing concern. It was important for children to have access to healthful milk, and so pasteurization was introduced in the United States in 1893. Unfortunately, many local purveyors of milk, to maximize their profits, diluted the milk with water. This, of course, would be noticeable, so to make the milk look white, they sometimes added chalk to it. To counter this, reformers saw to it that public milk stations were established where mothers could obtain wholesome milk for their children. Beginning in the early 1890s, New York, Boston, and Chicago began having medical inspectors perform annual checks of all school children, and by the early years of the twentieth century this practice had been instituted in sixty cities. Other actions included the opening of day nurseries, the establishment of children's wards in hospitals, and the organization of child welfare societies.

Based on ideas imported from Europe, attempts were made in several cities to form city-wide societies for the organization of charities, and by the early 1880s most of the large cities in the northeastern and north-central states contained such organizations. These organizations did not dispense relief, but rather investigated cases and compiled lists of needy families. By 1904 there were 150 these societies, many of which had been renamed associated charities. This period also saw the expansion of YMCAs and the establishment of YWCAs, as well as other organizations that did not have any religious affiliation. Still, most of these organizations were unable to deal with the problems that resulted from the depression following the Panic of 1893. A new approach to the problem of poverty was needed, and some thought that understanding the roots of poverty would help in finding a way to eradicate it.

Prominent among those taking this approach were the leaders of the social settlement movement. The inspiration for this movement came from England, and in particular, Toynbee Hall, which was founded in London in 1883. Most of the Americans involved were young college students, many of whom had spent some time at Toynbee Hall. Among the earliest of them were Stanton Coit, who organized the Neighborhood Guild in New York in 1886, and Vida D. Scudder, who was responsible for the College Settlement (1889), also in New York. Soon, similar centers were established in Boston and elsewhere. Another of the important leaders in the settlement-house movement was Jane Addams, who founded Hull House on Chicago's South Side. All of these institutions were established in the poor areas of the cities. The people who worked in them typically came from the middle and upper classes. They became residents of the settlement houses because it was believed that the only way to understand the problems of the poor was to live among them. It was hoped that a mutual understanding would develop, and that community problems could then be approached in a cooperative manner. The settlement houses offered many amenities for those who lived in their neighborhoods, and the settlement house leaders and residents often joined in local campaigns to improve the lives of the poor.

A logical venue for attacking social problems would appear to be through the churches, and the various religious denominations ultimately responded. At the outset of the period the Catholic Church was still not of major importance in most American communities, but it was significant in many large cities with substantial foreign-born populations. A large proportion of its parishioners were the poorest of immigrants, and the church did provide them with some assistance. However, it was only after some Protestant denominations established social and charitable activities that the Catholic Church, for fear of losing its communicants, expanded its own philanthropies. For the Jews, the synagogues and affiliated societies responded to social problems quite early. By the 1890s various Jewish groups began coordinating their activities. With the arrival of the East European Jews, who were very poor, these efforts were expanded. Felix Adler was a prominent Jewish social reformer who was concerned with education and housing, among other issues. His work inspired Rabbi Stephen Wise to begin the Free Synagogue movement, which was a Jewish version of the institutional church.

For years, Protestant churches were concerned about social problems, primarily because they considered them a threat to an orderly, moral life. They saw these problems arising as a result of the influx of poor immigrants, most of whom were Catholic. But since the poor immigrants were not their parishioners, many simply took the approach of moving out of deteriorating neighborhoods along with their middle- and upper-class congregations. By the 1870s, though, some Protestants concluded that poverty and the social problems that went along with it were the product of immoral lifestyles, and especially the consumption of alcoholic beverages. The result was a crusade for moral reform, and particularly a very vigorous temperance movement. But there were other Protestant clergymen who preached Christian responsibility for the welfare of fellow human beings, and they developed this into the concept of the Social Gospel. The clergymen who followed this became much more involved in the problems of the urban poor. Out of this came the development of what was known as the institutional church. Instead of the church only being a house of worship, these churches provided a variety of social services and amenities, such as medical clinics, athletic facilities, educational opportunities, and clubs and social activities. All the efforts by these various groups did not eliminate poverty or social problems, but much progress was made, especially in improving the lives of the underprivileged.

The Changing Appearance of Cities. By 1920 American cities looked vastly different than they had in 1860. To accommodate the great economic growth and tremendous population increase of those years, cities had expanded not only outward but, even more dramatically, upward. Formerly, churches and civic buildings had dominated the skyline; now the most prominent structures were office buildings, hotels and apartments, factories, and railroad stations. This new construction was aided by important advances in structural engineering. There also was more attention being paid to the design of aesthetically pleasing buildings.

To accommodate economic expansion more space was needed. Old firms were growing and new firms continually were being formed. It was desirable for business operations to be located in urban centers, especially New York, which became the principal administrative and banking center of the United States. But the downtown business districts were very crowded, and land was scarce and thus very expensive. Maximum utilization was necessary, and erecting tall buildings was the way to accomplish that. The result was that peculiarly American phenomenon know as the skyscraper. Before tall buildings could be erected, though, some technological breakthroughs were necessary. Obviously, no one would want to climb more than five or six flights of stairs, so the development of the elevator was very important. The first practical passenger elevator installed in a commercial building appeared in New York in 1857, but it was during this period that the elevator came into widespread use. New methods of construction also were essential. Traditionally, the weight of a building was supported by its walls. Tall buildings, therefore, would require very thick walls at the base, which would cut down on the usable space in the lower stories. With this construction method, the "skyscraper," in the modern sense, would be impossible. New materials—cast iron, and especially steel—and new construction techniques made the skyscraper feasible.

If we think of the skyscraper as not only a tall building, but also as one employing new structural techniques, its birthplace usually is considered to be Chicago; but economic necessity dictated that the earliest tall buildings were to be found in New York. The first of these was the office building of the Equitable Life Assurance Company, which was built between 1868 and 1870. While it may have seemed tall for its day, it was only 130 feet high, with five working stories. The architect primarily responsible was George B. Post, who also was the architect of the Western Union building (1873–75). This was a ten-story, 230 foot building. At about the same time the Tribune building was completed. This was a 260-foot structure, and it originally had ten stories, with nine more being added in 1905. A brick building, partially reinforced by an iron frame, it was the work of architect Richard M. Hunt. Neither the Western Union building nor the Tribune building was innovative structurally, however. More innovative was Post's Produce Exchange (1881–84). With eight stories and a height of 125 feet, this certainly was not a skyscraper, but it did utilize a structural system nearly like that necessary for a modern skyscraper.

The major breakthrough was the use of a metal skeleton to support the weight of a building. The man usually given credit for devising this method of construction is William LeBaron Jenney, a Chicago architect. The first building in which he employed this technique was the Home Insurance Company building (1885) in Chicago. In this ten-story building, the first six stories were supported by a wrought-iron frame, and the upper four stories by steel beams. This method of construction, in theory, made it possible to erect a building of almost any height. Also important, though, was the tremendous freedom it gave to the architect in designing the building. Since the walls no longer had to bear the weight of the building, but were really only there to keep out the elements, the architect had a far greater choice in the materials that could be used. For example, even such structurally weak materials as terra cotta or glass could be employed for a building's shell. Soon, other Chicago architects, Daniel H. Burnham, John W. Root, and Louis Sullivan, among them, were using this method. The first entirely steel-frame skyscraper was the second Rand McNally building in Chicago (1889–90), which was designed by Burnham and Root.

Chicago may have had the first modern skyscrapers, but it was New York that soon became most celebrated as a city of skyscrapers. One of New York's most famous skyscrapers is the twenty-one-story Flatiron Building, which was designed by the Chicago architect, Daniel H. Burnham, and completed in 1902. It quickly became a landmark because of its great height at that time, and because it has an interesting triangular shape. It is still one of New York's landmarks. By 1908, however, the Flatiron Building was overshadowed by the forty-one-story Singer Building, which rose 612 feet over Broadway. This was the world's tallest building, but it did not hold that title for very long. In 1913, the sixty-story Woolworth Building was completed. This 722-foot-high structure was to remain the tallest building in the world for nearly twenty years. The architect, Cass Gilbert, very successfully employed Gothic styling in this cathedral of commerce. Soon, the skyscraper became not only the symbol of New York and Chicago, but the symbol of the American big city. The symbolism was so strong, that even smaller cities aspired to civic greatness through the erection of tall buildings.

The appearance of America's cities changed not only because of their increasing vertical appearance, but also because from the late-nineteenth century to the beginning of World War I an effort was underway to do away with some of the ugliness that was wreaked upon the cities by unregulated economic expansion and growth. This effort was known as the "City Beautiful" movement. The World's Columbian Exposition, a great world's fair held in Chicago in 1893, was a very important catalyst to this movement, which had roots that predated the fair.

The backers of the fair were interested in producing a magnificent event that would boost Chicago, and in particular to demonstrate the progress the city had made since its disastrous fire in 1871. They put Daniel H. Burnham in charge of the fair, and chose Frederick Law Olmsted, America's foremost landscape designer, to lay out the grounds. The nation's leading architects were selected to design the fair buildings. Among them were Richard M. Hunt; McKim, Mead & White; and George B. Post of New York; and Louis Sullivan of Chicago. One of the most highly regarded sculptors of the time, Augustus Saint-Gaudens, was to advise on sculptural decoration. When they all met in Chicago to discuss design, Saint-Gaudens referred to it as "the greatest meeting of artists since the fifteenth century." Those assembled agreed that the architecture would be basically classical in design, that there would be a uniform cornice line, and that the color of the buildings would be white. The architects then modified their original sketches to conform to this plan. The only dissenter was Louis Sullivan. He had to accept the uniform cornice line, and he was forced to modify his original design to blend in with the overall theme, but his building, the Transportation Building, was the only nonclassical building in the main part of the fair. It also was the only building that was not white. The main focus of interest at the fair was the Court of Honor, which was a grouping of the fair's principal buildings around a large basin of water. What was created was a great "White City." The fair was very successful and well attended, and most Americans marveled at what they saw. The World's Columbian Exhibition had a tremendous impact on American architecture and city planning.

The effort toward urban beautification, which had begun before the fair, picked up speed. The White City, with its careful planning and classically inspired buildings, was seen as the image of what cities could be, and ambitious plans for beautification were launched in many cities. Architectural leagues and municipal art societies were formed to sponsor projects, and prizes were awarded for the best designs. The most dramatic effect could be seen in Washington, where it was decided to revive L'Enfant's plan for the city. Civic centers were planned, and in many cases were seen to completion. Grand boulevards were conceived, and the railroads erected magnificent railroad stations in major cities.

By 1920 the physical appearance of America's cities had changed so radically that many of them hardly would be recognizable to an observer from 1860. The church steeples that formerly had dominated the skylines, were seldom visible among the tall office towers. The mostly utilitarian structures that had housed public and private activities were now replaced by limestone or marble buildings inspired by the architecture of ancient Rome. While filth and slums, unfortunately, still existed, at least some of the ugliness occasioned by unregulated, rapid industrial expansion had been erased.

The Development of Urban Services. The rapidly growing cities of the United States faced many challenges during these years. Population expansion necessitated the laying out of many miles of new streets, which then had to be maintained. Businesses and individual households produced great quantities of garbage and trash that had to be removed. Older water supply systems no longer were adequate for the increasing needs of urban residents and businesses. The cities also had grown so large in area that they no longer could be traversed on foot, and so mass transportation systems needed to be instituted if the cities were to function. Taller buildings added new challenges to the task of preventing and fighting fires, and huge populations meant that police protection had to be expanded and regularized.

Although some cities in America had adequately paved streets, in most expansion had taken place so rapidly that many miles of streets remained unpaved. When streets were paved, the materials used varied considerably, and depended on local availability. Cobblestones were common, especially in Boston and Philadelphia. They had the advantage of being relatively inexpensive; but cobblestone streets were not easily cleaned, they were noisy, they were damaging to vehicles and uncomfortable for passengers riding in them. In New York, small granite blocks were used, and that material soon became popular for street surfacing in several eastern cities. In the Midwest, where stone was scarce, wooden blocks often were used. One problem with wooden blocks was that in wet weather they became "floating pavements," and so in time they were replaced by brick. Interestingly, asphalt, which was an excellent paving material that had been used in Paris after 1854 and in London after 1868, was not used in the United States until the 1870s. While it was generally believed that governments should do as little as possible, street paving was considered a governmental responsibility. Rather than use their own employees for the surfacing of streets, city governments usually looked to private contractors for this work. The awarding of these contracts often was accompanied by corruption. The work required great numbers of unskilled workers, and so it provided an area of employment for many members of immigrant groups.

At the beginning of this period most American cities were very dirty. The accumulation of garbage in many of New York's streets was so great that it was almost impossible to pass through them, and the sewers of New York emptied into the Hudson and East rivers. The streets of Philadelphia also were filthy, and many of them still were inhabited by pigs. That city's drinking water was taken from the Delaware River, into which the sewers emptied. In Baltimore, New Orleans, and Mobile, sewage ran through open trenches in the streets. Chicago and Milwaukee took their drinking water from Lake Michigan, and they also dumped their sewage into that lake. By the 1870s steps were being taken to deal with these unhealthy situations. Boston and New York began construction of mains to take the sewage away from the cities, and Chicago undertook a major engineering operation to try to solve their problem. The current of the Chicago River, into which the city dumped most of its waste, was reversed so that it flowed into the Illinois River instead of Lake Michigan. Gradually, municipalities assumed the responsibility of providing sewage facilities, and they financed the projects by selling bonds and assessing property owners.

New York made a substantial effort to improve sanitation after the 1895 appointment of George E. Waring as head of the Department of Street Cleaning. Waring began by trying to improve the morale of his department's workforce, and to call public attention to their work. His approach was to dress his employees in white uniforms, and to organize a parade of sanitation men in 1896. Cleaning the streets was one thing, but disposing of the waste was another, and more difficult, task. The practice had been to load the garbage on scows, tow them out to sea, and then dump it in the ocean. But the garbage did not always cooperate by sinking, and instead often was washed up on the beaches of Brooklyn, Long Island, and New Jersey. To rectify this problem, in 1896 Waring arranged to have a private contractor incinerate the city's garbage. At that time, this seemed like an acceptable solution to the problem.

Providing an adequate water supply increasingly had become a municipal responsibility in the nation's largest cities. Americans were very proud of the great water works of their cities, but as consumption rapidly increased there were fears that supplies soon would be inadequate. A growing population was one reason why water consumption increased, but it also was because Americans used water in far greater quantities than the people of any other country. The result of this was that cities constantly were looking for new sources for their water systems. In 1907 New York began the most ambitious project of this period when construction on the Catskill Aqueduct got underway. The aqueduct ran 120 miles from the Ashokan Reservoir in upstate New York to Staten Island. Water was distributed throughout the city by means of huge pressure tunnels that were hundreds of feet below street level.

It certainly was understood from the outset that it was important for the cities to ensure the purity of their water supplies. The problem was that there was disagreement as to what constituted pure water. At first water was judged by taste and clarity. Later, mineral content was tested, and it was believed that a low mineral content was most desirable. When water was subjected to examination under a microscope and tiny organisms were observed, some experts claimed that the water was unhealthy, but others disagreed. In any case, nothing was done about it. Obviously, though, dumping garbage or sewage into the sources of drinking water was not considered a very good thing to do, and so laws were passed prohibiting such action. Even though the filtration of water began in Paisley, Scotland in 1804, in the United States it was believed to be expensive and unnecessary, and so it was not until 1872 that Poughkeepsie, New York, became the first city in the nation to filter its water supply. In the 1890s major progress in filtering public water supplies was made in Massachusetts, and in the years that followed action was taken elsewhere. Chicago's earlier reversal of the Chicago River had not been working effectively, and the incidence of deaths from typhoid fever was exceptionally high. A sanitary district was created and a major engineering project was undertaken to build the Drainage Canal, which was opened in 1900. This may not have been very good for cities downstream, but in Chicago the typhoid death rate fell precipitously. Philadelphia, an early leader in providing a public water supply, did not provide the entire city with filtered water until 1911, but it was one of the first large cities to disinfect its water supply with liquid chlorine.

Major progress also was made in providing for urban mass transportation. At the beginning of the era, all urban motive power was provided by the horse. The major forms of urban transportation were horse-drawn omnibuses and street railways, but these were almost totally inadequate to the needs of these rapidly growing cities. Even though these vehicles crowded the streets of many cities, they were unable to handle the large numbers of people who had need of their services. In addition, they were slow moving, added to the filth of the streets, and were uncomfortable for their passengers. Because they had a very limited range, population mostly was confined to the center of the city, since without an effective means of urban transportation, workers had no choice but to live near where they worked. Clearly, new types of transportation were essential to the growth and progress of the cities of the United States.

As early as 1825 the idea of moving people around on elevated railways had been proposed as one way to deal with New York's transportation problems. The construction of an elevated railway was finally begun in 1867, and by 1870 a line was completed along Ninth Avenue as far north as Thirtieth Street. It was so successful, that it was proposed to extend it and also construct another line on Sixth Avenue. By 1878 the Sixth Avenue line had been built along most of the length of Manhattan. Other lines were planned, and ultimately built, into what were then the northern suburbs. During the next couple of decades elevated lines were built in Brooklyn, Kansas City, Chicago, and Boston. In reality, though, the elevated lines turned out to be a mixed blessing. While an efficient means of transportation, they also were unattractive, noisy, and expensive to build.

Another attempt to solve the urban transportation problem was the cable car. The cable car ran on tracks, and it received its motive power from an endless steel cable that was constantly moving below the ground. A mechanism on the cable car grabbed on to that cable, and thus was moved along. To stop the car, the cable would be released and a brake applied. The cable car originally was introduced in San Francisco in 1873, and it seemed to be a good system for moving people through that city's hilly streets. During the 1880s the cable cars began to run in the streets of Chicago, Philadelphia, and New York, and by the middle of the 1890s, there were hundreds of miles of cable car lines throughout the country. But there were some drawbacks. Most serious was the fact that a break in the cable would shut down the entire line until a repair could be made. Also, construction costs for a cable car system were quite high.

What seemed to be the answer to the urban transportation problem came with the development of electricity as a source of motive power. The greatest problem was to find a way to get the electric power to the engine. The solution was to do this by means of overhead wires, and the device that connected the vehicle to the electric wires was known as a trolley, a term that came to be applied to the vehicles themselves. The first of these electric trolleys was installed in Richmond in 1887–88. Trolley lines could be built and maintained at a reasonable cost, and they provided their passengers with transportation that was speedy and comfortable. By 1890 fifty-one cities had constructed trolley lines.

For all their advantages, though, the trolley lines did little to relieve the traffic congestion on city streets. The answer to that problem seemed to be to construct a transportation system that ran under the city streets. As early as 1868, Alfred Ely Beach built a 312-foot tunnel underneath New York's Broadway, in which he ran a pneumatic subway. It worked, and Beach wanted to extend the line; but he was unable to obtain a franchise bill from the state until 1873, and in that year of financial downturn, he found it impossible to raise the necessary money, and so the charter was withdrawn. It was not until the late 1890s that American cities turned to building subway systems, which already had been in use in London and Budapest. The first United States city to have subway service was Boston, which opened its initial unit in 1897. New York's first subway line began operation in October 1904, running on tracks that stretched nine miles from City Hall to 145th Street. A year later, trains were running under the East River to Brooklyn. The subway lines were built and owned by New York, but they were leased to private companies for operation.

For the most part, though, these various transportation systems were built and operated by private companies. Many of the promoters of these systems were less interested in making money from their operations, and more interested in using them as speculative ventures and as vehicles for stock watering and other devious activities. Before long, many miles of street railways were being operated by a national syndicate. Peter A. B. Widener and William L. Elkins soon controlled at least half of Philadelphia's street-car lines by 1884, and two years later they expanded their activities when they allied with Charles T. Yerkes and moved into Chicago. In New York William C. Whitney and Thomas Fortune Ryan moved into the traction business and formed a syndicate with Widener and Elkins. Before the century was over, this syndicate controlled street railways in New York, Philadelphia, Chicago, and many other cities.

The trolleys, elevated lines, and subways enabled the cities to expand in area. Because they could transport large numbers of people quickly and inexpensively, workers were now able to live farther from their places of employment, and inner-city congestion was somewhat abated. Still, these transit lines linked the newly developing areas of the cities with the downtown business districts and downtowns remained vital centers for commercial activity, retailing, and entertainment.

For the many American cities that were located on rivers, expansion meant being able to cross those rivers. Ferries were used early on, and their use continued; but bridges would be more efficient for moving large numbers of people and vehicles. Bridges had been built over the narrower rivers, but technological advances were necessary before the wider rivers could be spanned, and especially without interfering with river traffic. Such a project was completed in 1874, when the Eads Bridge (named for its designer, James B. Eads) crossed the Mississippi River at St. Louis. This was a double-decked, arched bridge that still carries vehicular traffic as well as both freight and passenger trains. For the cities of New York and Brooklyn spanning the East River, which had been proposed several times, became particularly important during the winter of 1866–67, when the weather became so severe that ferry service between the two cities was halted. In 1867 the New York Bridge Company was formed, and John Roebling, who unquestionably was the best man in his profession, was appointed as the chief engineer. Construction had barely gotten underway, when John Roebling died as a result of an accident at the site. The directors of the company appointed his son, Washington Roebling, to succeed him. He, too, was involved in an accident that, while not fatal, left him partially disabled. Nonetheless, he continued to supervise the construction of the bridge, using his wife as conduit to the workmen on the site. In the spring of 1883 the Brooklyn Bridge was opened to traffic. It was the longest suspension bridge in the world at that time. It immediately became heavily used, and its gothic-arched towers and vertical and diagonal cables gave it grace and beauty that inspired painters, photographers, writers, and poets over the years. New York and Brooklyn were now linked, and the bridge was the first step in the process that ultimately resulted in the consolidation of the two cities in 1898.

Fire Protection. The risks from fire increased not only because the cities were becoming more crowded, but also because of some new technologies such as illuminating gas and, later, electric wiring. In addition to presenting new risks for the starting of fires, they also presented challenges for extinguishing fires. Another challenge came as buildings grew taller, making it more difficult to evacuate people from those buildings. While small towns and the more backward cities continued to rely on volunteers for fighting fires, the larger cities, faced with these new conditions, were increasingly relying on professional fire companies.

Except for the steam pumper, fire-fighting equipment had not changed very much prior to the 1870s, but beginning in that decade many advances were made. Fire-alarm signal boxes and water towers to provide pressure were coming into use. Also during the 1870s the mechanical ladder truck was invented, and as buildings were growing taller it became widely adopted. In the 1880s chemical engines were introduced in several cities. With the development of the internal combustion engine, motorized fire trucks began to appear. There also were several advances made in reducing the danger of fire through the wider use of fire-resistant building materials and the 1877 invention of the automatic fire sprinkler. In general, American fire departments compared favorably with those of other countries.

Police Protection. The latter nineteenth century was a time of growing specialization and increased organization in many aspects of American life, and criminals were no exception to that trend. Those developments, coupled with an expanding urban population, meant that well-trained and efficient police forces were needed more than ever. However, by the end of the Civil War, only eight cities had uniformed police forces, and even though other cities established regular police forces in the ensuing years, police protection rarely was adequate.

Finding men who were willing to serve as policemen was not a problem, though. It was not always easy for unskilled laborers to find jobs, and the jobs they found were low paying and offered little security. On the other hand, police jobs paid well, sometimes as much as twice that of an unskilled laborer, and they usually were reasonably secure. Typically, there were more applicants for police jobs than there were positions to fill. Because these jobs were so desirable, political influence and money often determined who got them. Once employed, the policeman found that he was a part of a group that was separate from the rest of society. This was a result of the nature of police work, where hours were different from those of other workers. Policemen also spent a good deal of time either on the beat or in station houses. While most workers probably worked in the city in which they lived, that was especially true of policemen. And workers often changed employers, but policemen did not. Policemen had a great amount of power that ordinary citizens did not, which contributed to a "them" and "us" perception. Because policemen had a close and separate existence, police departments tended to hold on to tradition and frown upon innovation. Nonetheless, there were many improvements made in crime detection and law enforcement techniques. Alarm telegraphs, and later police telephones were introduced; mounted police were employed for crowd control, new methods of criminal identification were developed; and specialized detective forces were organized. Under Inspector Thomas Byrnes the Detective Bureau of the New York City Police Department became the most effective in the nation. Byrnes built a network of informers, made "treaties" with criminals to keep them out of the more affluent parts of the city, and employed the "third degree" to obtain information and confessions.

The nature of police work presented many opportunities for corruption. Probably no policeman exemplified corruption more than Alexander S. Williams of New York. Williams, who was better known as "Clubber" Williams, was transferred to the city's most fashionable red-light district in the early 1880s. Supposedly, when he learned of his transfer, he told a reporter that he had been living on salt chuck long enough, now he was going to get some of that tenderloin. Subsequently, that district became known as the "Tenderloin," and the name was applied to the principal vice districts of other cities. The graft Williams received from the brothels and gambling establishments made him a wealthy man. A decade after his transfer to the Tenderloin, he owned a town house in Manhattan, an estate in Connecticut, and a fifty-three-foot-long steam yacht. Several hundred formal complaints had been lodged against him and he had been fined more than two hundred times, but good political connections kept serious action from being taken against him; in fact, the 1887 report that listed all these complaints and fines also announced that he had been promoted from captain to inspector!

Conflicts between city and state helped establish a situation that furthered corruption. State legislatures were responsible for most vice legislation, and those legislatures were dominated by rural, protestant interests, who wanted the police to suppress vice. But the values of city dwellers often were different, and many of them did not rank prostitution and gambling high on their list of crimes. Enforcement, therefore, was selective, and police frequently took bribes to look the other way. The conflict between city and state also was political. Police departments were controlled by local political leaders in the middle of the nineteenth century, and the big city politicians usually were not of the same political party that dominated the rural areas of the state. The city politicians used the police to help maintain their control. Concerned with the corruption and the power of the big city politicians, several state legislatures took control of urban police forces beginning in the late 1850s. New York's police department was taken over by the state legislature in 1857, and the police of Baltimore, St. Louis, and Kansas City began to be operated by their states in the early 1860s. Boston's police department did not come under state management until 1885, but it was not returned to city control until 1962.

Urban Politics and Administration. Throughout this era, American municipal government was characterized by corruption, and whenever municipal corruption is mentioned, the name "Tammany" immediately comes to mind. This organization's roots go back quite far; it has existed in one form or another since 1787. In the beginning it was a nonpolitical fraternity, but gradually it became the political center of the Jeffersonian Republican party of New York County. In 1868 William M. Tweed took control of Tammany Hall, and usually is credited with creating the first urban political machine. Tweed was the first of the "bosses." Within a few years, his machine had looted perhaps $200 million from the city. The machine finally was exposed and turned out in 1871, but it took the combined efforts of the *New York Times* and cartoonist Thomas Nast of *Harper's Weekly*. Nast's cartoons proved to be especially devastating. Tweed supposedly remarked: "I don't care a straw for your newspaper articles, my constituents don't know how to read, but they can't help seeing them damned pictures." Tweed entered prison, and he died there of pneumonia in 1878. Other cities also had their bosses. In Philadelphia James McManes and the "gas ring" pretty much ran things, as did Christopher Magee in Pittsburgh. "Doc" Ames worked through a corrupt police department to run Minneapolis. In St. Louis it was Colonel "Ed" Butler, and in San Francisco the city government was controlled by "Blind Boss" Buckley.

The reasons for corruption were not immediately apparent and were rather numerous. Important, however, was the desire to make money and the emphasis placed on financial success. Great opportunities were available in the rapidly growing cities, especially arising out of the need to provide municipal services. Many people were willing to dispense bribes to cooperative city officials. And why not accept them? Society seemed neither to punish nor especially condemn the practice. After all, there was corruption in the national government, the state governments, and in business. For a skilled city boss it was fairly easy to get away with dishonesty. Cities had grown faster than their governments, resulting in a fragmentation of power and a breakdown in communications. The confused structure of city government often was unworkable. Somehow, though, the city had to function, and that is where the boss came in. The boss was someone who could get things done. Even if corruption was apparent, because of the confusion in government it was very difficult to determine who was responsible.

Poor immigrants formed an important segment of the power base of the boss. The boss was the poor man's friend. Most started out among the underprivileged, and usually they did not forget their roots. Working through a system of ward captains, the boss provided charity and jobs. Poor city dwellers knew they could go to their ward captains with their problems and often have them addressed. In return for these many favors, what was asked of the poor man? He was asked to provide the only thing he had to give—his vote. No matter that the boss was a thief, he did not steal from the poor. In a sense, the boss became a folk hero—a Robin Hood. But the immigrant was not the sole support of the boss. Cities that did not have large populations of newly arrived immigrants frequently were boss controlled, too. The urban middle and upper classes were just as much involved; they either supported the boss or looked the other way. The idea that municipal politics was by nature corrupt came to be pretty widely accepted. It was "dirty," and not to be touched by any respectable man, and certainly not by anyone with higher political ambitions. The bosses, of course, knew that they could not depend solely on the immigrants for support, and so they often catered to businesses, both legal and, sometimes, illegal businesses. Some of the more corrupt bosses even catered to the underworld.

For many poor immigrants and their children machine politics was one of the few ways they could achieve some wealth and community status. This especially was true of the Irish, who seemed well suited for politics. An advantage they had over other immigrant groups was knowledge of the English language. Also important was their attitude toward the English government in Ireland. Because they did not accept that formal government structure, they were used to working through an unofficial, informal government, which was not unlike some of the political machines in America's cities. New York, Boston, and several other American cities came to be dominated by Irish bosses. (*See Document No. 25.*)

Several historians have pointed out that while corruption was the stated issue in the battles to overthrow the bosses, a more significant issue was how the city should develop physically, and how much public money should be allocated to that expansion. Many of the reformers tended to be fiscal conservatives, and they advocated restrained growth. True, street paving, street lighting, sewer lines, and other municipal improvements were expensive, and the corrupt bosses could skim a good deal of money from them; but the citizens would have the advantage of those improvements. Reformers often would prefer that these projects not be undertaken, for fear that they would result in an increase of taxes.

Changing residential patterns also played a role in the movement for reform. Because of developments in transportation, many urban dwellers were able to leave the central city for residences in the outlying suburbs. But during the late-nineteenth and early-twentieth centuries cities frequently annexed these areas. As a result, these people remained residents of the city. They saw the inner city as the stronghold of the boss and his immigrant supporters, and while they lived outside the central city, they usually worked there. It was the residents of the peripheral areas who often were the leaders of the reform movement during the Progressive Era.

Many reform advocates came from the business community. They concluded that the problem lay in the structure of city government, and they wanted to change it to make it more efficient. The corporation was their model, and they wanted to separate politics from administration and make use of experts, rather than elected officials. Aided by the National Municipal League, which was formed in 1894, they put forward a program that included freeing cities from state control, focusing municipal responsibility, reducing opportunities for corruption, reforming election procedures, and having governments run by experts. Despite the appearances of a broadening of democracy, these reformers often advocated centralizing decision making. One way their goals were achieved was through the institution of city manager and commission forms of government. The commission form of government was first adopted in Galveston, Texas, in 1901. This form of government was turned to after Galveston's old government was unable to function during a tidal wave and storm in September 1900. Under it, the city was placed under the control of five elected commissioners, four of whom headed city departments, and the fifth, the mayor-president, coordinated the other four. That government was very successful, and within a decade a hundred other communities adopted it.

The idea that running a city was like running a business gave rise to a new form of government known as the city-manager type. Under this system, an expert administrator was hired by the city council or commission to run the city, and the council or commission played a role similar to the board of directors of a corporation. This form of government proved to be popular, and by 1912 it had been adopted by 210 communities. Two questions might be raised: Is the city analogous to a business? Can it be run by non-political "experts"?

During the Progressive Era there also were some other reformers who were elected to office, and who were not primarily concerned with structural reform, but were more interested in social reform. One of the earliest of these was Hazen S. Pingree, who was elected mayor in Detroit in 1889. He served in that position for seven years before he was elected as Michigan's governor. Like the bosses, Pingree built a political machine that derived much of its support from the foreign born; but unlike many of them, Pingree fought corruption and worked for the public good. He was especially notable for his fights with the street railways and gas companies, and for establishing a municipal electric lighting plant. In fact, Pingree came to be a very early advocate of municipal control of utilities. Samuel M. "Golden Rule" Jones was one of the most colorful of the late-nineteenth-century mayors. A wealthy businessman, he became mayor of Toledo in 1897. Like Pingree, he was an advocate of public ownership of utilities, and he also favored abolishing the private contract system for carrying out city work. Among Jones's accomplishments were instituting the eight-hour day for city employees, and establishing free kindergartens in the public schools and public playgrounds for children. Another successful businessman who became a social reformer was Thomas L. Johnson, who was elected mayor of Cleveland in 1901, and held that office for eight years. During those years, the city took over the street railways and reduced the fare to 3 cents. Unlike many other reformers who came from the upper classes, these mayors were not particularly concerned with regulating working-class morals, and so they were not inclined to take action against Sunday drinking, gambling, or prostitution, nor were they likely to support restrictive blue laws.

If these reform mayors took on some of the aspects of the bosses, there also were some bosses who supported reform and promoted the careers of a number of honest, liberal, reform-minded politicians. Did these bosses really believe in reform? The question is irrelevant. What they really believed in was retaining power, and doing so meant pleasing their constituents. If their constituents supported reform measures, so too did the savvy bosses. In looking at municipal government and politics, it is much too simplistic to equate "reform" with good, or "boss" or "machine" with bad.

PART II

DOCUMENTS

DOCUMENT NO. 1

DESCRIPTION OF BOSTON IN 1663*

The Englishman, John Josselyn, first visited Boston in 1638, only eight years after it was founded. When he returned in 1663, he found a much more mature settlement that clearly had taken on most of the characteristics associated with urban life, as can be seen from this description.

γ   γ   γ

. . . the houses are for the most part raised on the Sea-banks and wharfed out with great industry and cost, many of them standing upon piles, close together on each side the streets as in *London*, and furnished with many fair shops, their materials are Brick, Stone, Lime, handsomely contrived, with three meeting Houses or Churches, and a Town-house built upon pillars where the Merchants may confer, in the Chambers above they keep their monethly Courts. Their streets are many and large, paved with pebblestone, and the South-side adorned with Gardens and Orchards. The Town is rich and very populous, much frequented by strangers, here is the dwelling of their Governour. On the North-west and North-east two constant Fairs are kept for daily Traffick thereunto. On the South there is a small, but pleasant Common where the Gallants a little before Sun-set walk with their *Marmalet*-Madams, as we do in *Morefields*, &c. till the nine a clock Bell rings them home to their respective habitations, when presently the Constables walk their rounds to see good order kept, and to take up loose people. . . . the Harbour before the Town is filled with Ships and other Vessels for most part of the year.

* Source: John Josselyn, *An Account of Two Voyages to New-England: Wherein You Have the Setting Out of a Ship, with the Charges, the Prices of All Necessaries for Furnishing a Planter and His Family at His First Coming, a Description of the Countrey, Natives, and Creatures, with Their Merchantil and Physical Use, the Government of the Countrey As It Is Now Possessed by the English, &c., a Large Chronological Table of the Most Remarkable Passages, From the First Discovering of the Continent of America, to the Year 1673*, 162–63.

DOCUMENT NO. 2

WILLIAM PENN'S INSTRUCTIONS FOR THE ESTABLISHMENT OF PHILADELPHIA*

William Penn conceived the City of Philadelphia as central to his plans for his Pennsylvania colony. In his instructions to his commissioners who were to accompany the first settlers, he not only provided details for laying out its principal city, but also stipulated that purchasers of land in the colony were to receive city lots in proportion to their holdings.

γ   γ   γ

I.   That so soon as it pleaseth God that the above persons arrive there, a certain quantity of land or ground plat shall be laid out for a large town or city, in the most convenient place upon the river for health and navigation; and every purchaser and adventurer, shall, by lot, have so much land therein as will answer to the proportion which he hath bought or taken up upon rent. But it is to be noted, that the Surveyors shall consider what roads or highways will be necessary to the cities, towns, or through the lands. Great roads from city to city not to contain less than forty feet in breadth, shall be first laid out and declared to be for highways, before the dividend of acres be laid out for the purchaser, and the like observation to be had for the streets in the towns and cities, and there may be convenient roads and streets preserved, not to be encroached upon by any planter or builder, that none may build irregularly to the damage of another. . . .

II.   That the land in the town be laid out together after the proportion of *ten thousand* acres of the whole country; that is *two hundred* acres, if the place will bear it: However, that the proportion be by lot, and entire, so as those that desire to be together, especially those that are by the catalogue laid together, may be so laid together both in the town and country. . . .

V.   That the proportion of lands that shall be laid out in the first great town or city, for every purchaser, shall be after the proportion of ten acres for every *five hundred* acres purchased, if the place will allow it.

* Samuel Hazard, ed., *Hazard's Register of Pennsylvania, Devoted to the Preservation of Facts and Documents, and Every Kind of Useful Information Respecting the State of Pennsylvania*, 16 Vols. (Philadelphia: W. F. Geddes [1828–35].), 1:324–25.

DOCUMENT NO. 3

THE PLANNING CONCEPT FOR THE NATION'S CAPITAL*

Pierre Charles L'Enfant, a Frenchman who volunteered to serve in the American army under George Washington, and who rose to the rank of major, was selected to draw the plan for the nation's capital. He discussed his concept and grand vision in these 1791 letters to Washington.

γ　　　　　　γ　　　　　　γ

In viewing the intended establishment in the light and considering how in process of time a city so happily situated will extend over a large surface of ground, much deliberation is necessary for to determine on a plan for the total distribution and . . . that plan [should be conceived] on [such] a system . . . as to render the place commodious and agreeable to the first settler, [while] it may be capable of . . . [being] enlarged by progressive improvement . . . [all] which should be foreseen in the first delineation in a grand plan of the whole city combined with the various grounds it will cover and with the particular circumstance of the country all around.

In endeavoring to effect this, it is not the regular assemblage of houses laid out in squares and forming streets all parallel and uniform that it is so necessary, for such a plan could only do on a level plain and where no surrounding object being interesting it becomes indifferent which way the opening of streets may be directed.

But on any other ground, a plan of this sort must be defective, and it never would answer for any of the spots proposed for the Federal City, and on that held here as the most eligible it would absolutely annihilate every [one] of the advantages enumerated and. . . . alone injure the success of the undertaking.

Such regular plans indeed, however answerable they may appear upon paper or seducing as they may be on the first aspect to the eyes of some people must even when applied upon the ground the best calculated to admit of it become at last tiresome and insipid and it never could be in

* Elizabeth S. Kite, *L'Enfant and Washington, 1791–1792: Published and Unpublished Documents Now Brought Together for the First Time* (Baltimore: The Johns Hopkins University Press, 1929), 47–48, 53–54.

its origin but a mean continuance of some cool imagination wanting a
sense of the real grand and truly beautiful only to be met with where
nature contributes with art and diversifies the objects.

In a subsequent letter L'Enfant discusses the concept of his plan.
My whole attention was directed to a combination of the general distribution of the several situations, an object which, being of almost immediate
moment, and importance, made me sacrifice every other consideration—
and here again must I solicit your indulgence, in submitting to your
judgment—my ideas, and in presenting to you a first drawing, correct
only as it respects the situation and distance of objects, all which were
determined and well ascertained having for more accuracy had several
lines run upon the ground cleared of the wood, and measured with
posts fixed at certain distances to serve as bases from which I might
arrange the whole with a certainty of making it fit the various parts of
the ground.

Having determined some principal points to which I wished to make
the others subordinate, I made the distribution regular with every street
at right angles, North and south, east and west, and afterwards opened
some in different directions, as avenues to and from every principal
place, wishing thereby not merely to contract with the general regularity,
nor to afford a greater variety of seats with pleasant prospects, which
will be obtained from the advantageous ground over which these avenues are chiefly directed, but principally to connect each part of the city,
if I may so express it, by making the real distance less from place to
place, by giving to them reciprocity of sight and by making them thus
seemingly connected, promote a rapid settlement over the whole extent,
rendering those even of the most remote parts an addition to the principal, which without the help of these, were any such settlement attempted, it would be languid, and lost in the extent, and become detrimental to the establishment. Some of these avenues were also necessary
to effect the junction of several roads to a central point in the city, by
making these roads shorter, which is effected [by directing them] to
those leading to Bladensburg and the Eastern branch—both of which
are made above a little shorter, exclusive of the advantage of their leading immediately to the wharves at Georgetown. The hilly ground which
surrounds that place the growth of which it must impede, by inviting
settlements on the city side of Rock Creek, which cannot fail soon to

spread along all those avenues which will afford a variety of pleasant rides, and become the means for a rapid intercourse with all parts of the city, to which they will serve as does the main artery in the animal body, which diffuses life through the smaller vessels, and inspires vigor, and activity throughout the whole frame.

These avenues I made broad, so as to admit of their being planted with trees leaving 80 feet for a carriage way, 30 feet on each side for a walk under a double row of trees, and allowing ten feet between the trees and the houses.

DOCUMENT NO. 4

COMMENTS ON LOUISVILLE, 1819*

To Henry McMurtrie, a physician and an early observer of Louisville, the flaws in that city's plan were obvious, and he drew attention to some of their consequences. On the other hand, he was very much impressed with Louisville's commercial progress, and he predicted future growth.

γ   γ   γ

Louisville's Plan

Two great faults in the plan of this town must be evident to the most superficial observer. The one is a want of alleys, the other that of public squares. With respect to the first, much inconvenience is already the consequence, and what that will increase to when the population will amount to 20,000 souls, (a period not far distant,) may be readily conceived. It is not yet, however, too late to correct this error, and as the sacrifice of a few feet of ground in each lot would add greatly to the present and future value of it, self-interest, will I have no doubt, soon cause it to be attempted.

The total want of public squares, is an evil of much more serious cast, and one that promises hereafter to furnish full employment to the sons of Esculapius [*sic*] and their suite. Rapidly as this town augments its

---

* Henry McMurtrie, *Sketches of Louisville and Its Environs* (Louisville: S. Penn, Jr., 1819), 114, 193.

population, a few years will find every foot of ground within its pre-
cincts covered with houses, forming ramparts that will keep without,
that ministering angel of health, a pure and circulating atmosphere, and
keep within, the daemon of contagion, who draws his very existence
from the foul and pestilent airs of a pent up city.

Commerce

The increase of the navigation and commerce of Louisville and Ship-
pingport, since the year 1806, is, perhaps, unparalleled in the history of
nations. At that time, six keel boats and two barges, the one of thirty
tons, belonging to Reed, of Cincinnati, the other of forty, owned by In-
stone, of Frankfort, sufficed for the carrying trade of the two places,
whereas at the present moment, there are (exclusive of barges, keels,
&c.) upwards of twenty-five steam boats employed in that business,
whose united burthen is equal to six thousand and fifty tons!—This is
a flattering and unequivocal proof of their prosperity, and gives us a
glimpse of what they will be fifty years hence.

DOCUMENT NO. 5

OHIO RIVER CITIES, 1815*

*Daniel Drake, an eminent physician of his time, arrived in Cincinnati at
the age of fifteen, and remained there for the rest of his life. He became that
city's most prominent resident, and was the author of numerous scientific
works. The volume from which this excerpt is taken was modeled on a similar
study of Philadelphia, which had been published four years earlier. Here he
comments on what he envisions for the future for the Ohio River cities of
Pittsburgh, Louisville, and, especially, Cincinnati.*

γ   γ   γ

Where will be erected the chief cities of this promising land? It may be
answered with certainty—on the borders of the Ohio river. They are not
likely to become places of political importance, for these must lie towards the centres of the states which this river will divide; but the com-

* Daniel Drake, *Natural and Statistical View, or Picture of Cincinnati and the Miami
Country* (Cincinnati: Looker and Wallace, 1815), 228–32.

mercial and manufactural advantages that exist in lieu of the political, are so much superior, as to justify, in this enquiry, the omission of every town not situated on the Ohio. Pittsburgh, Cincinnati and Louisville, are the places which at present have the fairest prospects of future greatness. The age of Cincinnati is intermediate to the others. Their population and business correspond at present with the order of their enumeration; but the time is apparently not remote, when a different comparative rank will be assigned them. Both Cincinnati and Louisville seem destined to surpass Pittsburgh. To this prediction the inhabitants of that town—for thirty years the *entrêpot* of all the Ohio countries—are not expected to assent. It will even be regarded by them, as groundless and arrogant; but without stopping to anticipate and repel the charges of self interest and vain glory, I shall proceed to a brief exposition of the relative advantages of that town and this. It is well known to all the people of the United States, that for twenty years, both foreign and Atlantic goods, to the amount of several millions of dollars, have been annually waggoned [*sic*] to Pittsburgh, deposited in its warehouses, and shipped in its boats for the country below. The expense of these operations has, of course, been defrayed by the consumers in Kentucky, Tennessee, Ohio, and the adjoining Territories, who have thus made to the prosperity of Pittsburgh a yearly contribution of great value. Hundreds of our merchants were passing, moreover, through this town; and it was early discovered, that if manufactures were established, it would be possible to dispose of many articles required in the newer settlements below. Hence founderies [*sic*], glass houses, breweries, and iron manufactories of various kinds, were erected; and the wares of this "Birmingham of America" superadded to the merchandise of the East, soon spread extensively over our country. During such a period of commercial prosperity, the borough could not but flourish; and were the causes of its growth as permanent as they have been efficient, it would unquestionably retain an enviable superiority. But a change in the current of our importations—such a change as has already begun—must inevitably reduce the ratio of improvement in that place, just as much as it will be increased by the same cause, in Cincinnati, Louisville and the other towns below. The waggoners employed in the transportation of our merchandise from Philadelphia; the boat builders and commission merchants; the freighters, and those who manufacture for these populous young states, will no longer receive our specie for their services; and must of course find other employments, or emigrate to other towns.

The coal and iron of that place will indeed long continue abundant; but these are easily floated with the current to the towns below; which can thus establish the manufactures dependent on these important articles with nearly as much facility as they are set up in Pittsburgh—while that town must obtain its cotton and sugar, its hemp and lead, at an expense of freightage, taking these articles together, more than twice as great as that paid by us. The country around that place is moreover, rugged and sterile, in comparison with that about either Cincinnati or Louisville; and the greatest population it can support, will have a correspondent rarity. Pittsburgh, therefore has not so high a destination as its younger rivals to the westward; but it must forever maintain a very important and respectable rank.

The chief advantage which Louisville posseses over Cincinnati, is the partial interruption of commerce at that place by the *Falls* of the Ohio. The cargoes of boats, when the water is low, are waggoned for two miles round those rapids. This not only gives employment to a great number of hands, but it makes the town one of the heads of navigation—a place of debarkation and deposit—where, of course, an active mercantile business may be done. If these obstructions to the navigation were irremoveable, Louisville would certainly arrive at a very exalted degree of commercial greatness. But the opinion of professional engineers is such as to dissipate much of this interesting prospect. The desired improvement was actually commenced more than a year ago; and altho' the prosecution of it has been for some time suspended—by causes not necessarily connected with the undertaking—there can be no doubt of its being resumed, and finished before the lapse of many years. When this is done, the commercial importance of that town must receive a signal reduction; but still it will possess the peculiar advantage of a site for great water works. It will, moreover, be the emporium of an extensive and fruitful district in Kentucky; for which its situation on a southern bend of the Ohio gives it a number of advantages. Still there are reasons for believing that CINCINNATI IS TO BE THE FUTURE METROPOLIS OF THE OHIO. Its *site* is more eligible than that of most towns on the river. It is susceptible of being rendered healthier than Louisville, and is extensive enough for a large city. The Ohio bounds it on the south-east, south, and south-west, so that all the streets, if extended, would at one or both ends, intersect the river within the limits of the corporation. It has, therefore, a great extent of shore, along the whole of which there is not a reef nor shoal to prevent the landing of boats. Opposite to Broadway, is the mouth of the Licking; a river whose navigation will certainly be much improved. Over the town plat . . . a canal at some future period may be conducted from the Great Miami; whose waters can, by another canal, be connected with those of the Maumee, and thus secure to us a new and profitable trade with the lakes. A survey of the Ohio will exhibit to us the important fact, that between Pittsburgh and Louisville there is not a single spot, where a future rival to Cincinnati can be raised up. Finally, by a reference to the map of the Miami country, it may be seen that the river, in approaching Cincinnati from Maysville, which is 60 miles above, runs generally to the north-west; that after passing the town, it soon alters its course, and flows nearly to the south for more than 40 miles; and consequently, that Cincinnati lies in a situation to command the trade of the eastern and western, as well as the interior portions of the Miami country. This is the case for more than 30 miles in those directions; and when the improvement of the roads shall be such as to facilitate intercourse with this place, the power it must exercise over these opposite districts will be still greater. The adjoining parts of Kentucky, altho' politically disconnected, must long continue to acknowledge their commercial dependence on Cincinnati. Thus, it is the permanent mart and trading capital of a tract whose area equals the cultivable portion of New-Hampshire, New Jersey or Maryland; surpasses the state of Connecticut, and doubles the states of Rhode Island and Delaware taken together—with a greater quantity of fertile and productive soil, than the whole combined.

These are some of the local advantages of Cincinnati; and if improved with a spirit corresponding to their magnitude, its inhabitants cannot fail to realize their most glowing anticipations of future greatness.

DOCUMENT NO. 6

LOWELL, MASSACHUSETTS IN 1842*

The novels of the eminent English author, Charles Dickens, were very widely read in the United States. In 1842 Dickens traveled to America to go on the lecture circuit, capitalizing on his popularity and earning money to make up for royalties he did not receive on his books when issued by American publishers. He was familiar with factory towns in England, and he was very

---

* Charles Dickens, *American Notes for General Circulation* (London: Chapman and Hall, 1850), 45–48.

interested in visiting Lowell, an American manufacturing city. There, he
found an industrial center that stood in marked contrast to those of his native
country.

γ   γ   γ

I was met at the station at Lowell by a gentleman intimately connected with the management of the factories there; and gladly putting
myself under his guidance, drove off at once to that quarter of the town
in which the works, the object of my visit, were situated. Although only
just of age—for if my recollection serve me, it has been a manufacturing
town barely one-and-twenty years—Lowell is a large, populous, thriving place. Those indications of its youth which first attract the eye, give
it a quaintness and oddity of character which, to a visitor from the old
country, is amusing enough. It was a very dirty winter's day, and nothing in the whole town looked old to me, except the mud, which in some
parts was almost knee-deep, and might have been deposited there, on
the subsiding of the waters after the Deluge. In one place, there was a
new wooden church, which, having no steeple, and being yet unpainted,
looked like an enormous packing-case without any direction upon it. In
another there was a large hotel, whose walls and colonnades were so
crisp, and thin, and slight, that it had exactly the appearance of being
built with cards. I was careful not to draw my breath as we passed, and
trembled when I saw a workman come out upon the roof, lest with one
thoughtless stamp of his foot he should crush the structure beneath
him, and bring it rattling down. The very river that moves the machinery in the mills (for they are all worked by water power), seems to ac-
quire a new character from the fresh buildings of bright red brick and
painted wood among which it takes its course; and to be as light-headed,
thoughtless, and brisk a young river, in its murmurings and tumblings,
as one would desire to see. One would swear that every "Bakery," Gro-
cery," and "Bookbindery," and other kind of store, took its shutters
down for the first time and started in business yesterday. The golden
pestles and mortars fixed as signs upon the sun-blind frames outside the
Druggists', appear to have been just turned out of the United States'
Mint; and when I saw a baby of some week or ten days old in a woman's
arms at a street corner, I found myself unconsciously wondering where
it came from: never supposing for an instant that it could have been born
in such a young town as that.

There are several factories in Lowell, each of which belongs to what we should term a Company of Proprietors, but what they call in America a corporation. I went over several of these; such as a woollen factory, a carpet factory, and a cotton factory: examined them in every part; and saw them in their ordinary working aspect, with no preparation of any kind, or departure from their ordinary every-day proceedings. I may add that I am well acquainted with our manufacturing towns in England, and have visited many mills in Manchester and elsewhere in the same manner.

I happened to arrive at the first factory just as the dinner hour was over, and the girls were returning to their work; indeed the stairs of the mill were thronged with them as I ascended. They were all well-dressed, . . . and that phrase necessarily includes extreme cleanliness. They had serviceable bonnets, good warm cloaks, and shawls; and were not above clogs and patterns. Moreover, there were places in the mill in which they could deposit these things without injury, and there were conveniences for washing. They were healthy in appearance, many of them remarkably, and had the manners and deportment of young women: not of degraded brutes of burden. If I had seen in one of those mills (but I did not, though I looked for something of this kind with a sharp eye), the most lisping, mincing, affected, and ridiculous young creature that my imagination could suggest, I should have thought of the careless, moping, slatternly, degraded, dull reverse (I have seen that), and should have been still well pleased to look upon her.

The rooms in which they worked, were as well ordered as themselves. In the windows of some, there were green plants, which were trained to shade the glass; in all, there was as much fresh air cleanliness, and comfort, as the nature of the occupation would possibly admit of. Out of so large a number of females, many of whom were only then just verging upon womanhood, it may be reasonably supposed that some were delicate and fragile in appearance: no doubt there were. But I solemnly declare, that from all the crowd I saw in the different factories that day, I cannot recall or separate one young face that gave me a painful impression; not one young girl whom, assuming it to be a matter of necessity that she should gain her daily bread by the labour of her hands, I would have removed from those works if I had the power.

They reside in various boarding-houses near at hand. The owners of the mills are particularly careful to allow no persons to enter upon the possession of these houses, and whose characters have not undergone the most searching and thorough inquiry. Any complaint that is made against them, by the boarders, or by any one else, is fully investigated; and if good ground of complaint be shown to exist against them, they are removed, and their occupation is handed over to some more deserving person. There are a few children employed in these factories, but not many. The laws of the State forbid their working more than nine months in the year, and require that they be educated during the other three. For this purpose there are schools in Lowell; and there are churches and chapels of various persuasions, in which the young women may observe that form of worship in which they have been educated.

At some distance from the factories, and on the highest and pleasantest ground in the neighbourhood, stands their hospital, or boarding-house for the sick: it is the best house in those parts, and was build by an eminent merchant for his own residence. Like that institution at Boston, which I have before described, it is not parcelled out into wards, but is divided into convenient chambers, each of which has all the comforts of a very comfortable home. The principal medical attendant resides under the same roof; and were the patients members of his own family, they could not be better cared for, or attended with greater gentleness and consideration. The weekly charge in this establishment for each female patient is three dollars, or twelve shillings English; but no girl employed by any of the corporations is ever excluded for want of the means of payment. That they do not very often want the means, may be gathered from the fact, that in July, 1841, no fewer than nine hundred and seventy-eight of these girls were depositors in the Lowell Savings Bank: the amount of whose joint savings was estimated at one hundred thousand dollars, or twenty thousand English pounds.

I am now going to state three facts, which will startle a large class of readers on this side of the Atlantic very much.

Firstly, there is a joint-stock piano in a great many of the boarding-houses. Secondly, nearly all these young ladies subscribe to circulating libraries. Thirdly, they have got up among themselves a periodical called The Lowell Offering, "A repository of original articles, written exclusively by females actively employed in the mills,"—which is duly printed, published, and sold; and whereof I brought away from Lowell four hundred good solid pages, which I have read from beginning to end.

The large class of readers, startled by these facts, will exclaim, with one voice, "How very preposterous!" On deferentially inquiring why, they will answer, "These things are above their station." In reply to that objection, I would beg to ask what their station is.

It is their station to work. And they *do* work. They labour in these mills, upon an average, twelve hours a day, which is unquestionably work, and pretty tight work too. Perhaps it is above their station to indulge in such amusements, on any terms. Are we quite sure that we in England have not formed our ideas of the "station" of working people from accustoming ourselves to the contemplation of that class as they are, and not as they might be? I think that if we examine our own feelings, we shall find that the pianos, and the circulating libraries, and even the Lowell Offering startle us by their novelty, and not by their bearing upon any abstract question of right or wrong. . . .

Of the merits of the Lowell Offering as a literary production, I will only observe, putting entirely out of sight the fact of the articles having been written by these girls after the arduous labours of the day, that it will compare advantageously with a great many English Annuals. It is pleasant to find that many of its Tales are of the Mills and of those who work in them; that they inculcate habits of self-denial and contentment, and teach good doctrines of enlarged benevolence. A strong feeling for the beauties of nature, as displayed in the solitudes the writers have left at home, breathes through its pages like wholesome village air, and though a circulating library is a favourable school for the study of such topics, it has very scant allusion to fine clothes, fine marriages, fine houses, or fine life. . . .

In this brief account of Lowell, and the inadequate expression of the gratification it yielded me, and cannot fail to afford to any foreigner to whom the condition of such people at home is a subject of interest and anxious speculation, I have carefully abstained from drawing a comparison between these factories and those of our own land. Many of the circumstances whose strong influence has been at work for years in our manufacturing towns have not arisen here; and there is no manufacturing population in Lowell, so to speak: for these girls (often the daughters of small farmers) come from other States, remain a few years in the mills, and then go home for good.

The contrast would be a strong one, for it would be between the Good and Evil, the living light and deepest shadow. I abstain from it, because I deem it just to do so. But I only the more earnestly adjure all those whose eyes may rest on these pages, to pause and reflect upon the difference between this town and those great haunts of desperate misery; to call to mind, if they can in the midst of party strife and squabble, the efforts that must be made to purge them of their suffering and danger: and last, and foremost, to remember how the precious Time is rushing by.

DOCUMENT NO. 7

MANUFACTURING IN CINCINNATI*

The noted Scottish publisher, William Chambers, toured the United States from September through mid-December of 1853. A man of great curiosity and intelligence, Chambers's observations are more detailed and perceptive than most travel writers of his time. He was especially fascinated by the growth of cities in what was then the American West. Here, he writes about the commercial and industrial growth of Cincinnati.

γ   γ   γ

Placed on the Ohio, 1600 miles from the ocean, steamers are seen at the quay of Cincinnati, taking on board freight and passengers for New Orleans, and all other places of importance on the Mississippi, and its larger tributaries. Vessels of less burden proceed up the Ohio to Wheeling and Pittsburg [*sic*], whence there is now a communication by railway with Philadelphia and Baltimore; and keeping in recollection the ready access by railway and canal to Cleveland, on Lake Erie, it will be seen that Cincinnati is the centre of a circle which bears on the Atlantic in the east, the vast prairies on the west, the lake-countries on the north, and the Gulf of Mexico on the south. It is only by a perception of this wide and comprehensive radius, with its enormous and ever-accumulating demand for products of mechanical industry, that we can understand the character of those manufacturing establishments which are making Cincinnati one of the wonders of the New World—and which, after all, are nothing to what they must ultimately become when the population of the great West is consolidated.

When one thinks of a carpenter's shop, he has probably in his mind two or three rude-looking apartments, with at the most a dozen men in paper-caps working at benches with planes and chisels, or leaning over

* William Chambers, *Things As They Are in America* (London and Edinburgh: W. and R. Chambers, 1854), 150–56.

a plank with a hand-saw; or with experience a little more extended, he may perhaps get the length of fancying a cabinet-making establishment with fifty picked hands turning out several handsome pieces of furniture daily. The idea of a factory as large as a Lancashire cotton-mill for making chairs, tables, or bedsteads by machinery, would hardly present itself to his imagination. Yet, it is on this factory-mill system that we find house-furniture produced in Cincinnati. Curious to see such places, I spend a day in rambling about the outskirts of the city, where manufactories of various kinds are conducted upon a scale that went very far beyond my previous notions of what can be done by machinery.

The first establishment I visited was a furniture-factory—a huge brick building, five stories in height, with a long frontage at the corner of two streets, and in which 250 hands are employed in different departments. Many of these are occupied merely in guiding and superintending machines moved by shafts and belts from a large steam-engine on the ground-floor. Every article receives its shape in the rough, by means of saws; and these move with such rapidity, that their teeth are invisible to the eye. The articles are next planed, or turned, and morticed, in the same inconceivably rapid manner. In the planing operations, some surprising effects are produced. A rough deal, or other piece of wood, being arranged on a bench under the action of a plane which revolved horizontally, was in a few instants smoothed as if by the finest hand-labour. Chairs of a common class, but neatly turned and painted, were the principal article of manufacture. The number produced almost goes beyond belief. I was informed that the average quantity was 200 dozen every week, or at the rate of 124,800 chairs per annum, worth from five to twenty-four dollars per dozen. Among these, a large number are rockers. The machinery for scooping out and shaping the seats was exceedingly ingenious. The next article in importance is chests of drawers, of which 2000 are manufactured annually. Baby-cribs are another important item; but the number of them produced could not be definitely stated. . . .

The next establishment I looked in upon was a bedstead factory, in which similarly improved machinery was employed to cut out and finish various parts of the articles required. As many as 1000 bedsteads are turned out every week, valued at from four to twenty-four dollars each. Some other works were visited, but it is undesirable to enter on details respecting their products. In the fabrication of iron stoves, locks and hinges, window-frames, ornamental cabinet-ware, upholstery, firearms, hats, boots and shoes, machinery, axes and other edge-tools, carriages and numerous other things—the operations were on a similarly gigantic scale. . . . .Where do all these manufactures go? Of course the explanation is found in the perpetual demand over the vast regions of which, as has been said, Cincinnati is the centre. Every day, thousands of fresh families are making a settlement in the wilderness, and each needs bed-steads, tables, chairs, and other articles of domestic use. On the quay at Cincinnati, therefore, you see vast piles of new furniture, iron stoves, tinware, cases of boots and shoes, and everything else needed by set-tlers, preparing to be dispatched a thousand miles by steamers on the Mississippi and its tributaries. One manufacturer of cabinet-work told me he had received an order to make the whole furniture of a hotel in California! . . .

The most curious thing of all about Cincinnati, is its system of pig-killing and pork-pickling. The place is known as the principal hog-market in the United States. The hogs are reared in the country around on the refuse of the corn-fields after harvest, and among the extensive forests, where they pick up food at little or no cost to their owners. Brought in steamers from a great distance, they are seen marching and grunting in large herds through the streets to the slaughtering estab-lishments in the neighbourhood. The season in which they begin to make their appearance is the fall, when they are in prime condition, and when, from the state of the temperature, their carcasses can soon be cooled by the air, and rendered fit for pickling. The greater number of the hog slaughter-houses are behind the town, on the road towards the higher grounds, and are generally wooden structures of a very plain de-scription. Each is provided with a series of pens, whence the animals walk in single file along an enclosed gallery towards the apartment where they meet their doom.

When a pig is killed in England, the sufferer usually takes care to let the whole neighbourhood hear of the transaction. On such occasions, it is the prescriptive right of the pig to squeak, and he is allowed to squeak accordingly. In Cincinnati, there is no time for this. Impelled along the passage from the exterior pen, each hog on entering the chamber of death receives a blow with a mallet on the forehead, which deprives him of consciousness and motion. The next instant he is bled to death; and by means of an extensive system of caldrons and other requisites, the carcass is speedily cleaned, dressed, and hung up to undergo the proper cooling, previous to being cut in pieces and pickled.

DOCUMENT NO. 8

EMPLOYMENT LIMITATIONS FOR
NORTHERN BLACKS*

*Thomas Hamilton was a British army officer turned writer, who publish-
ed a then very popular, but now totally obscure, novel in 1827. From October
1830 until July 1831 he toured the United States. His resulting two-volume
travel diary,* Men and Manners in America, *was one of the most widely
read of the time. He was critical of several American institutions, especially slavery. In December of 1830 he decided to take time to visit some of
New York's educational institutions, among them the African Free School
No. 2. The dedicated and perceptive teacher he questioned most likely was
Charles C. Andrews, a white man, who published a history of that school in
the same year.*

γ   γ   γ

It has often happened to me, since my arrival in this country, to hear
it gravely maintained by men of education and intelligence, that the Ne-
groes were an inferior race, a link as it were between man and the brutes.
Having enjoyed few opportunities of observation on people of colour in
my own country, I was now glad to be enabled to enlarge my knowledge
on a subject so interesting. I therefore requested the master to inform
me whether the results of his experience had led to the inference, that
the aptitude of the Negroe children for acquiring knowledge was inferior to that of the whites. In reply, he assured me they had not done so;
and, on the contrary, declared, that in sagacity, perseverance, and capacity for the acquisition and retention of knowledge, his poor despised
scholars were equal to any boys he had ever known. "But alas, sir!" said
he, "to what end are these poor creatures taught acquirement, from the
exercise of which they are destined to be debarred, by the prejudices of
society? It is surely but a cruel mockery to cultivate talents, when in the
present state of public feeling, there is no field open for their useful employment. Be his acquirements what they may, a Negroe is still a Negroe, or, in other words, a creature marked out for degradation, and ex-

---

* Thomas Hamilton, *Men and Manners in America*, 2 Vols. (Edinburgh: W. Blackwood,
1833), 1:91–98.

121

clusion from those objects which stimulate the hopes and powers of other men."

I observed, in reply, that I was not aware that, in those states in which slavery had been abolished, any such barrier existed as that to which he alluded. "In the State of New York, for instance," I asked, "are not all offices and professions open to the man of colour as well as to the white?"

"I see, sir," replied he, "that you are not a native of this country, or you would not have asked such a question." He then went on to inform me, that the exclusion in question did not arise from any legislative enactment, but from the tyranny of that prejudice, which regarding the poor black as a being of inferior order, works its own fulfilment in making him so. There was no answering this, for it accorded too well with my own observations in society, not to carry my implicit belief.

The master then proceeded to explain the system of education adopted in the school, and subsequently afforded many gratifying proofs of the proficiency of his scholars. One class were employed in navigation, and worked several complicated problems with great accuracy and rapidity. A large proportion were perfectly conversant with arithmetic, and not a few with the lower mathematics. A long and rigid examination took place in geography, in the course of which questions were answered with facility, which I confess would have puzzled me exceedingly, had they been addressed to myself.

I had become so much interested in the little party-coloured crowd before me, that I recurred to our former discourse, and enquired of the master, what would probably become of his scholars on their being sent out into the world? Some trades, some description of labour of course were open to them, and I expressed my desire to know what these were. He told me they were few. The class studying navigation, were destined to be sailors; but let their talents be what they might, it was impossible they could rise to be officers of the paltriest merchantmen that entered the waters of the United States. The office of cook or steward was indeed within the scope of their ambition; but it was just as feasible for the poor creatures to expect to become Chancellor of the State, as mate of a ship. In other pursuits it was the same. Some would become stonemasons, or bricklayers, to the extent of carrying a hod, or handling a trowell, the course was clear before them; but the office of master-bricklayer was open to them in precisely the same sense as the Professorship of Natural Philosophy. No white artificer would serve under a coloured master. The most degraded Irish emigrant would scout the idea with indignation. As carpenters, shoemakers, or tailors, they were still arrested by the same barrier. In either of the latter capacities, indeed, they might work for people of their own complexion, but no *gentleman* would ever think of ordering garments of any sort from a *schneider* of cuticle less white than his own. Grocers they might be, but then who could conceive the possibility of a respectable household matron purchasing tea or spiceries from a vile "Nigger?" As barbers, they were more fortunate, and in that capacity might even enjoy the privilege of taking the President of the United States by the nose. Throughout the Union, the department of domestic service peculiarly belongs to them, though recently they are beginning to find rivals in the Irish emigrants, who come annually in swarms like locusts.

On the whole, I cannot help considering it a mistake to suppose, that slavery has been abolished in the Northern States of the Union. It is true, indeed, that in these States the power of compulsory labour no longer exists; and that one human being within their limits, can no longer claim property in the thews and sinews of another. But is this all that is implied in the boon of freedom? If the word mean anything, it must mean the enjoyment of equal rights, and the unfettered exercise in each individual of such powers and faculties as God has given him. In this true meaning of the word, it may be safely asserted that this poor degraded caste are still slaves. They are subjected to the most grinding and humiliating of all slaveries, that of universal and unconquerable prejudice. The whip, indeed, has been removed from the back of the Negro, but the chains are still on his limbs, and he bears the brand of degradation on his forehead. What is it but mere abuse of language to call him *free*, who is tyrannically deprived of all the motives to exertion which animate other men? The law, in truth, has left him in that most pitiable of all conditions, *a masterless slave*.

It cannot be denied, that the Negro population are still compelled, *as a class*, to be the hewers of wood, and the drawers of water, to their fellow citizens. *CITIZENS!* there is indeed something ludicrous in the application of the word to these miserable Pariahs. What privileges do they enjoy as such? Are they admissible upon a jury? Can they enroll themselves in the militia? Will a white man eat with them, or extend to them the hand of fellowship? Alas! If these men, so irresistibly manacled to degradation, are to be called *free*, tell us, at least, what stuff are slaves made of!

DOCUMENT NO. 9

HOMES OF PROSPEROUS NEW YORKERS*

One of the most interesting and perceptive travel diaries of the 1850s was that written by Isabella Lucy Bird, an Englishwoman who visited te United States in 1854. Her observations on how Americans lived, especially those of some means, are of particular value. In this passage she describes in detail the homes of prosperous New Yorkers.

γ   γ   γ

The magnificence of the private dwellings of New York must not escape mention, though I am compelled to withhold many details that would be interesting, from a fear of "violating the rights of hospitality." The squares, and many of the numbered streets, contain very superb houses of a most pleasing uniformity of style. They are built either of brown stone, or of dark red brick, durably pointed, and faced with stone. This style of brick masonry is extremely tasteful and beautiful. Every house has an entrance-porch with windows of stained glass, and double doors; the outer one being only closed at night. The upper part of the inner door is made of stained glass; the door-handles and bell-pulls are made of highly-polished electro-plate; and a handsome flight of stone steps, with elegant bronze balustrades, leads up to the porch. The entrance-halls are seldom large, but the staircases, which are of stone, are invariably very handsome. These houses are six stories high, and usually contain three reception-rooms; a dining-room, small, and not striking in appearance in any way; as dinner-parties are seldom given in New York; a small, elegantly-furnished drawing-room, used as a family sitting-room, and for the reception of morning visitors; and a magnificent reception-room, furnished in the height of taste and elegance, for dancing, music, and evening parties.

In London the bedrooms are generally inconvenient and uncomfortable, being sacrificed to the reception-rooms; in New York this is not the case. The bedrooms are large, lofty, and airy; and are furnished with all the appurtenances which modern luxury has been able to devise. The profusion of marble gives a very handsome and chaste appearance to

* Isabella Lucy Bird, *The Englishwoman in America* (London: John Murray, 1856), 355–59.

these apartments. There are bath-rooms generally on three floors, and hot and cold water are laid on in every story. The houses are warmed by air heated from a furnace at the basement; and though in addition open fires are sometimes adopted, they are made of anthracite coal, which emits no smoke, and has rather the appearance of heated metal than of fuel. Ornamental articles of Parisian taste and Italian workmanship abound in these houses; and the mouldings, cornices, and woodwork, are all beautifully executed. The doorways and windows are very frequently of an arched form, which contributes to the tasteful appearance of the houses. Every species of gaudy decoration is strictly avoided; the paint is generally white, with gilt mouldings; and the lofty rooms are either painted in panels, or hung with paper for a very simple pattern.

The curtains and chair-covers are always of very rich damask, frequently worth from two to three guineas a yard; but the richness of this, and of the gold embroidery, is toned down by the dark hue of the walnut-wood furniture. The carpets of the reception-rooms are generally of rich Kidderminster, or velvet pile; an air of elegance and cleanliness pervades these superb dwellings; they look the height of comfort. It must be remembered that the foregoing is not a description of a dwelling here and there, but of fifty or sixty streets, or of 4000 or 5000 houses, those inhabited by merchants of average incomes, storekeepers not of the wealthiest class, and lawyers. The number of servants kept in such mansions as these would sound disproportionately small to an English ear. . . .

Having given a brief description of the style of the ordinary dwellings of the affluent, I will just glance at those of the very wealthy, of which there are several in Fifth Avenue, and some of the squares, surpassing anything I had hitherto witnessed in royal or ducal palaces at home. The externals of some of these mansions in Fifth Avenue are like Apsley House, and Stafford House, St. James's; being substantially built of brown stone. At one house which I visited in —— street, about the largest private residence in the city, and one which is considered to combine the greatest splendour with the greatest taste, we entered a spacious marble hall, leading to a circular stone staircase of great width, the balustrades being figures elaborately cast in bronze. Above this staircase was a lofty dome, decorated with paintings in fresco of eastern scenes. There were niches in the walls, some containing Italian statuary, and others small jets of water pouring over artificial moss.

There were six or eight magnificent reception-rooms, furnished in various styles—the Mediaeval, the Elizabethan, the Italian, the Persian, the modern English, &c. There were fountains of fairy workmanship, pictures from the old masters, statues from Italy, "*chefs d'oeuvre*" of art; porcelain from China and Sèvres; damasks, cloth of gold, and *bijoux* from the East; Gobelin tapestry, tables of malachite and agate, and "knick-knacks" of every description. In the Mediaeval and Elizabethan apartments, it did not appear to me that any anachronisms had been committed with respect to the furniture and decorations. The light was subdued by passing through windows of rich stained glass. I saw one table the value of which might be about 2000 guineas. The ground was black marble, with a wreath of flowers inlaid with very costly gems upon it. There were flowers or bunches of fruit, of turquoise, carbuncles, rubies, topazes, and emeralds, while the leaves were of malachite, cornelian, or agate. The effect produced by this lavish employment of wealth was not very good. The bedrooms were scarcely less magnificently furnished than the reception-rooms; with chairs formed of stag-horns, tables inlaid with agates, and hangings of Damascus cashmere, richly embossed with gold. There was nothing gaudy, profuse, or prominent in the decorations or furniture; everything had evidently been selected and arranged by a person of very refined taste.

DOCUMENT NO. 10

A BOSTON HOTEL, 1850*

The great American luxury hotels frequently were described by British visitors to the United States. One of them, Marianne Finch, stayed at the Revere House during her 1850 visit to Boston. Her travel diary provides many details about the accommodations and operation of that hotel, as well as a rather amusing description of a dinner in the hotel dining room. While her comments on the quality of the food served generally are negative—probably because many of the items were not familiar to her—it is clear that less finicky guests would not leave the table hungry.

* Marianne Finch, *An Englishwoman's Experience in America* (London: R. Bentley, 1853), 12–16.

γ   γ   γ

On Arriving at the Revere hotel, I was shown into a very large, and elegantly-furnished drawing-room, while my father went to the office to enter our names, and secure bed-rooms. This house is considered by many the best in the States; and when I left the country I was of that opinion too. I staid at the Astor House in New York, and some others as large and as elegantly fitted up; but I never experienced anything like a *home* feeling in any except the "Revere," which I attribute, in a great measure, to the perfect order and excellent arrangement of this establishment. The servants are very pleasant and obliging; and, if you choose, you may live as retired as in your own house; although (at that time) there were four hundred and fifty guests in it, an average of one hundred and twenty arriving, and the same number departing, daily. From one hundred and thirty to one hundred and fifty servants are kept, with a book-keeper, and a staff of clerks, in the office. These particulars I received from the house-steward, who took a party of us through the establishment. There are three dining-rooms; that appropriated to ladies, and gentlemen accompanying them, is two hundred and thirty feet long; the gentlemen's ordinary is larger. These rooms, and the passages, are warmed by pipes filled with steam. The drawing-rooms and bed-rooms have open fires, as with us.

The charge is two dollars (or 8s. 4d. English) per day, including board, lodging, and servants. Washing is extra, and rather an expensive item: one dollar a dozen, with exceptions; for instance, a nightcap, with an extra border, is charged a quarter of a dollar. 1s. 0 ½ d. I paid for the washing of a nightcap! Read that, ye Liverpool washers at 8d. a-dozen and be comforted; for there is a country where washing meets with its reward.

Hotel living is on the same plan everywhere, varying in cleanliness and comfort. The price is generally from one dollar and a-half to two dollars and a-half per day, taking your meals at a public table. Breakfast is served in summer at seven, half an hour later in the winter, at which there is everything that can be thought of. The dinner-hour varies from twelve to five. At this meal there is an infinite variety of dishes, and a larger number of persons than at breakfast. Tea, which is similar to breakfast, finishes the day.

It is a great advantage to a stranger to be brought in contact with so many persons of both sexes, without any trouble. As a traveller, I prefer this system to our plan of private rooms; but as to their boasted good living, I would rather have a good English beef-steak, or mutton-chop, than the choicest American viands.

The hour for dining is come. The gong sounds. The company enter, and take their seats with a gravity befitting the occasion. There is nothing on the table but vegetables, hashes, and bills of fare. The first waiter makes a sign—the vegetables are bared before you, the waiters carrying off the covers triumphantly. Presently they reappear, each armed with two plates of soup, with which they challenge the company. I accept one (as the warmest thing I am likely to get), and generally manage to overcome it. After a little skirmishing with the soup-plates, the battle begins in earnest. Plates of beef, mutton, pork, and beans, brought from a side table, are attacked and annihilated in no time. Ducks, geese, chickens, turkeys, and waiters, are flying about in all directions. I ask for a little turkey,—receive a piece of the leg (nearly cold), with a great deal of sweet and sour sauce. I leave it in disgust, and ask for beef,—find it tough and tasteless; I try the mutton, which proves worse. I repudiate both. What is called "green corn" is served up: it is Indian corn, boiled as a vegetable, when young. Tomatoes are not tolerable; squash is not attractive as a vegetable. There is nothing left but indifferent potatoes; with these I struggle till the first waiter makes another sign. A truce follows. The cold and empty dishes are borne solemnly away, and the reserved *corps* is brought on the table. The strife is renewed, but with less vigour than heretofore: still, considerable havoc is made among creams, custards, fruit, pastry, and especially squash-pies. For some time I was deterred from tasting the latter, on account of the name: it reminded me so of killing cock-roaches. However, one day, having been completely foiled in the first course, I determined to overcome my prejudice and attack the squash-pie. "What's in a name?" said I; "plum-pudding, by any other name, would taste as good." This remembrance of the pudding was almost too much for my resolution; but I persevered, and my virtue was rewarded. The squash-pie was very good. I have often fallen back upon it since, when discomfited in every other quarter. I do not say this with any wish to find fault with, or change, the order of things here. I have no doubt a well-regulated appetite would enjoy American dainties very much.

DOCUMENT NO. 11

THE STREETS OF NEW ORLEANS*

The filthy streets of New Orleans were noted frequently by visitors to the Crescent City. James Robertson, an Englishman who was there in January of 1854, described the unsanitary conditions and noted a foul odor in the air, leaving the reader to imagine how much worse it might be in hot weather.

γ   γ   γ

The streets are the dirtiest I had ever seen. The sewers are all open, and though drained into Lake Pontchartrain, yet, as there is but little fall, they are generally half full of stagnant water, and mud, and the refuse of the streets. From the river, a current of water is directed nightly along the sewers (ditches?) of the streets running towards the lake, and this serves to carry off much of the loose refuse; but in those which run along the streets parallel to the river and lake, no arrangements have been made to keep them clean; and it is only when there happens to be a fall of rain, that they receive a thorough purification. In consequence of this neglect, the water in those sewers, in less than four-and-twenty hours after rain, becomes covered with a dirty green crust, and even at this season of the year—in winter—gives off a most offensive smell. In the evenings, when the air is moist, this is peculiarly disagreeable and unhealthy.

The streets are now and again raked, for the accumulation of rubbish is too great to be removed by sweeping, but the refuse thus collected is often permitted to remain in the middle of the streets for one or two days; and if, in the interval, there happen to be a heavy fall of rain, those heaps are washed down, and their contents again carried into the sewers.

* James Robertson, *A Few Months in America: containing remarks on some of its Industrial and Commercial Interests* (London: Longman, [1855]), 63.

DOCUMENT NO. 12

INHABITANTS OF CHARLESTON STREETS*

Another English visitor to America's shores, John Benwell, was struck by the animal inhabitants of Charleston's streets during his sojourn there in 1853. The buzzards, in particular, often caught the attention of travelers stopping at Charleston.

γ   γ   γ

As you walk the streets of Charleston, rows of greedy vultures, with sapient look, sit on the parapets of the houses, watching for offal. These birds are great blessings in warm climates, and in Carolina a fine of ten dollars is inflicted for wantonly destroying them. They appeared to be quite conscious of their privileges, and sailed down from the house-tops into the streets, where they stalked about, hardly caring to move out of the way of the horses and carriages passing. They were of an eagle-brown colour, and many of them appeared well conditioned, even to obesity. At night scores of dogs collect in the streets, and yelp and bark in the most annoying manner. This it is customary to remedy by a gun being fired from a window at the midnight interlopers, when they disperse in great terror. I should remark that this is a common nuisance in warm latitudes. Some of these animals live in the wilds, and, like jackals, steal into the towns at night to eke out a scanty subsistence. At first my rest was greatly disturbed by their noisy yelpings, but I soon became accustomed to the inconvenience, and thought little of it.

---

* J[ohn] Benwell *An Englishman's Travels in America: His Observations of Life and Manners in the Free and Slave States* (London: Binns and Goodwin [1853]), 203–4.

DOCUMENT NO. 13

FIGHTING FIRES*

There were many things about the United States that fascinated Thomas Wilson, an 1859 visitor from England, but he devoted considerable attention to describing the manner in which American cities dealt with the menace of fire. This passage from his travel diary focuses especially on fire fighting in New York.

γ   γ   γ

The organisation of the New York Fire department is the most complete that could be adopted for the purpose; and the necessity for such an organisation may be estimated when I mention, that in one year (1858) alone there were two hundred and sixty-one fires there, involving losses to the amount of $1,108,646. The city is divided into eight fire districts, and each district has its own alarm-bell. In the event of a fire occurring, the bell in that particular district sounds the alarm: If in No. 1 district, the bells sound once, if in No. 2 twice, if in No. 3 three times, and so on; the bell-man next gives notice by means of an electric wire, with which all the bell towers communicate, to the central police office, and thence the alarm is conveyed to all the other fire bells in the city; the alarm then becomes general, all the bells striking the number of times corresponding with the number of the district in which the fire is situated. By this means, in the course of a very few minutes all the firemen in the town are on the alert, and the confusion which would result in case the precise locality were unknown is obviated. The force of the Fire department consists of fourteen engineers, and eighteen hundred and fifty members of engine companies, twelve hundred and fifty-seven members of hose companies, and four hundred and fifty-two members of hook and ladder companies; making a total of three thousand five hundred and fifty-nine men, with numbers on the increase. The above are divided into forty-eight engine, sixty hose and fifteen hook and ladder companies. There are in good working order at present fifty engines, forty-three hose carriages, eleven hook and ladder trucks, and forty-two hose tenders.

* Thomas Wilson, *Transatlantic Sketches: or, Travelling Reminiscences of the West Indies and United States* (Montreal: John Lovell, 1860), 132–36.

The companies of the fire brigade are generally composed of young active artisans; and there is great emulation amongst the different companies as to their efficiency and the respectability of their appearance in case of fires, or on gala days. Each company has its own uniform, very often consisting of a red flannel jacket or shirt, a strongly protected water proof hat, drab trousers and large jack boots. The companies are generally provided with an engine from the corporation, but more frequently they purchase one for themselves.

These engines are decorated in very handsome style, and often hundreds of dollars are spent in this way on a favorite machine; the hose carriages are also gorgeously ornamented with silver-plated lamps, &c. these machines are light carriages on two wheels, capable of carrying nine lengths of hose, each length being fifty feet; these are wound round a roller between the wheels; and immediately one end to the hose is screwed on to the hydrant, the carriage moves away until the whole of the hose is wound off. The engine also generally carries a couple of lengths; all the hose are made the same diameter, so as to allow of their being easily fitted together; at present there are about seventy thousand feet of hose in good working order.

The Fire department of New York City is conducted upon the Volunteer system, in contradistinction to Boston and some other towns, where the members receive one hundred dollars per annum each; every fireman provides his own uniform, &c., this costs $25 and upwards according to the taste or means of the wearer. In some of the companies' houses there are beds for the men, so that in case of an alarm during the night, they may be on the alert.

The engine houses are suitably fitted up with all necessary appliances, and in many cases ornamented with pictures and portraits of those members whose acts of daring have rendered them conspicuous among their comrades. Frequently badges of different companies, from all parts of the Union, may be seen gracing the walls; these have been presented as marks of attention from members who have been the recipients of civilities. The badges which are the distinguishing mark of the different fire companies, are often applied to uses for which they were not intended; sometimes, falling into the hands of unprincipled persons, they are used to gain admittance to fires for the purpose of pillage, but I am happy to say that instances of this kind are rare.

Viewing the various fire departments as they exist in almost every

town of the Union, I must admit that the public spirit which had undertaken their organisation is only equalled by the vigour which has carried it out, and the success which has attended their efforts; at the same
time it cannot but be a matter of regret that there is so much of the
rowdy element intermixed with what is of essential importance to the
community at large. Not unfrequently instances occur of rival companies rushing down to fires with revolvers, not even concealed, attached
to their persons. Quarrels, easily provoked, lead to the use of these
weapons; and instead of endeavouring to assist at the preservation of life
and property to which their duty calls them, they are engaged in deadly
strife with one another. I remember one evening in Philadelphia being
present at one of these rencontres, where two of the firemen were shot
and thirteen persons amongst a crowd of others who had assembled at
the alarm of fire, were seriously wounded. Although these scenes are
often caused by *rowdies* attacking the firemen, yet too frequently they
occur amongst rival companies; and if, as in the case I mention at Philadelphia, the companies in fault were totally disbanded, I think it would
act in a salutary manner of the majority of the force.

DOCUMENT NO. 14

SAN FRANCISCO, 1869*

*In 1869 Samuel Bowles, a newspaper editor from Springfield, Illinois,
published an account of his recent travels from the Mississippi River to the
Pacific Ocean. He predicted a prosperous future for several new cities, such
as Denver and Omaha, but no city seemed to him more likely to achieve
major status than San Francisco.*

γ   γ   γ

The population of San Francisco is now about one hundred and fifty
thousand, which is nearly one-third that of the whole State. Commerce
and manufactures are the great interests of the town; and the growth of
both is now very rapid. Already the third, San Francisco will speedily

---

* Samuel Bowles, *Our New West: Records of Travel between the Mississippi River and the
Pacific Ocean* (Hartford, CT: Hartford Publishing Co., 1869), 356–57, 360–61.

rank as the second commercial city of the Republic; about forty ocean steamers go and come in her waters,—to China and Japan, Mexico, Sandwich Islands, Oregon, British Columbia, and Panama; and over three thousand sailing vessels entered her Bay in 1868. Most of the latter are employed in the coast trade for lumber, coal and grain; but the importation of merchandise from Europe and the Atlantic States, and exportation of wheat and wool in return, have employed a large fleet of first-class ships. . . .

Location, surroundings, climate, facilities, these briefly sketched beginnings, all give certain assurance of a grand future for San Francisco. Never, does it seem, were such elements of sure and rapid growth gathered over another city, as now gather about this. What London is to Central and Western Europe, what New York is to the Atlantic States, that certainly San Francisco will be to the Pacific Coast region. Then she is nearer that great store-house of population and wealth, Asia, than either of her rivals. She has a nearer and more various agriculture, also, than either can boast of. She is the center and seaport of the great mineral-producing region of the continent, of the world. Our East, Europe, Asia will alike come to her for gold and silver and for wheat. What greater evidence of her advantage and their dependence, than this simple fact. Her population is more likely to treble than to double in ten years; and wonderful as the changes upon these sand-hills in the twenty years since gold was discovered in California, still more complete and revolutionary will those of the next ten years be.

Even now San Francisco will impress all her visitors deeply in many ways. They will see it is very new; yet they will find it is very old. Civilization is better organized here in some respects than in any city out of Paris; some of its streets look as if transplanted from a city of Europe; others are in the first stages of rescue from the barbaric desert. Asia, Europe and America have here met and embraced each other; yet the strong mark of America is upon and in all; an America, in which the flavor of New England can be listed above all other local elements; an America in which the flexibility, the adaptability, and the all-penetrating, all-subduing power of its own race , are everywhere and in everything manifest.

DOCUMENT NO. 15

DENVER AND TOURISM*

Over a period of four years Edward Hungerford, an American, visited many cities in the United States in an effort to discover their "personalities." His descriptions, several of which appeared earlier in magazines, were gathered in a book first published in 1913. He comments here on the tourist industry in Denver.

γ   γ   γ

Tourists form no small portion of Denver industry. She has restaurants and souvenir shops, three to a block; seemingly enough high-class hotels for a town three times her size. Yet the restaurants and the hotels are always filled, the little shops smile in the sunshine of brisk prosperity. And as for "rubberneck wagons," Denver has as many as New York or Washington. They are omnipresent. The drivers take you to the top of the park system, to the Cheesman Memorial, to see the view. All the time you are letting your eyes revel in the glories of those great treeless mountains, the megaphone man is dinning into your ears the excellence of his company's trips in Colorado Springs, in Manitou, in Salt Lake City. He assumes that you are a tourist and that you will have never had enough.

Tourists become a prosperous industry in a town that has no particular manufacturing importance. Great idle plants, the busy smelters of other days, bespeak the truth of that statement. Denver, as far as she has any commercial importance, is a distributing center. Her retail shops are excellent and her wholesale trade extends over a dozen great western states. Her banks are powers, her influence long reaching. But she is not an industrial city.

---

* Edward Hungerford, *The Personality of American Cities* (London: Grant Richards, 1914), 270–71.

DOCUMENT NO. 16

CHICAGO'S ECONOMY*

Walter G. Marshall, an Englishman, traveled to the United States in 1879, with the intention of writing a book about his observations. He referred to Chicago as a "marvellous city," and he wrote of its position as a great commercial and industrial city. His attention was drawn to the meatpacking industry, in particular.

γ   γ   γ

It is to its supreme position as a commercial centre that Chicago owes its prosperity. Lying at the south-west corner of Lake Michigan, at the head of the navigation of the great inland lakes—a seaport several hundred miles from the sea, yet in direct water communication with the Atlantic; with some of the most fertile and productive lands in the whole country stretching for hundreds of miles to the south and west of it; with a perfect network of railways opening out of these immense tracts, all converging at this point; the natural depôt for the unloading and re-shipping of endless cargoes of grain and other produce, as well as of "lumber," shingles, coal, iron, salt, etc., that come pouring into the place daily by water and by rail; the primary market in America, if not in the world, for the receipt of livestock, of hogs and oxen to be slaughtered and boxed, of cattle, sheep and hogs to be shipped alive to different parts of the country, and to other countries as well; the central market, in short, of a grand agricultural, food-producing country, Chicago has a position which is simply unrivalled; and when we think of the illimitable resources of the vast extent of country to the westward, of the lands to be peopled, of the soil to be cultivated and rendered productive, of the mining and other industries which will in time be developed, it seems that Chicago is destined sooner or later to take its stand as one of the very foremost cities on the face of the globe.

As a livestock market Chicago is pre-eminently famous. The Union Stock Yards, lying on the outskirts of the city, have capacity for holding 147,000 head, namely 100,000 hogs, 25,000 cattle, 22,000 sheep; and there are stalls besides for 500 horses. The sight when I visited this mar-

* W[alter] G. Marshall, *Through America: or, Nine Months in the United States* (London: Sampson Low, Marston, Searle, & Rivington, 1882), 88–93.

ket of such an immense number of animals herded together in the pens, the miles of water-troughs and feed-troughs, the bustle and confusion caused by the hundreds of drovers who were looking after their stock which had lately come in by the trains from distant parts of the State, and from places beyond, and who mingled their shouts with the lowing of the oxen and the bleating of the sheep, of which there were thousands, was one to be ever remembered. . . . .

Adjoining the Union Yards are the great pork and beef packing-houses, which are thirty in number, where the slaughtering of hogs and oxen is prosecuted on a mammoth scale—where as may as 80,000 can be "handled" during the course of a single day. The number of hogs packed here in 1872 amounted to, in round numbers, 1,900,000, and 1,781,900 during the year 1875. I was once taken over to the slaughter-house of the Anglo-American Packing company,—it was in September, 1879,—and I watched how Mr. Porker was put through his facings. Two thousand hogs had just come in to be slaughtered—that was the number to be dressed on the day of my visit; but I was told by one of the super-intendents that sometimes as many as from 7000 to 8000 are packed by this company daily. There is one house where 20,000 animals can be slaughtered and dressed in one day. The process the pig has to go through is as brief as it can be made. . . . Each animal takes about fifteen minutes to go through the whole operation, from the time that he is first swung up into the air till he is dangling skinless, headless, "intestine-less" in the hanging-room waiting to get cooled so that he may be prop-erly seasoned and boxed. One hog after another is despatched in this way as fast as can be managed. More than 4,000,000 head of pork were packed in Chicago in six years, from 1872 to 1877 inclusive. There were 4,805,000 hogs slaughtered here in 1879.

As an important grain market the Queen City is scarcely less famous. In 1872 she was the recipient of 88,426,842 bushels of breadstuffs (flour, wheat, barley, Indian corn, rye, and oats), of which 83,364,324 bushels were shipped. Even this is far exceeded by the receipts of 1879, which reached the amazing total of 137,624,833 bushels, including 62,164,238 bushels of Indian corn alone: and yet this, again, is only 3,538,238 bush-els in excess of the receipts of 1878. The shipments in 1879 amounted to 129,851,553 bushels. For receiving the grain and transferring it to the railway waggons when it is brought in by ship, immense towers or "elevators" (of corrugated zinc), twenty in number, have been set up along the shore of Lake Michigan, and they have a storage capacity of

16,000,000 bushels. Some of them are eighty feet high or more. They unload at the rate of about 7000 bushels an hour each.

As a market for one more important article of commerce, Chicago stands unrivalled, and that is for "lumber," or timber for industrial purposes, such as is used in the construction of houses, for flooring, mouldings, doors, sashes, blinds, etc. The total quantity of pine lumber received at this port in 1879 by water and rail—as I find by the annual report of the Chicago Lumbermen's Association—reached 1,467,720,091 feet, an increase of 287,735,381 feet, or about twenty-five per cent. over the receipts of any previous year in the history of the trade. This added to what remained over in the city yards from the year 1878, namely 410,773,000 feet, brings the aggregate supply for 1879 to 1,878,493,091 feet. The average increase in the receipts of lumber at this market has been at the rate of about 50,000,000 feet per year.

One might continue giving facts and figures like these to show the enormous interests which this wonderful city has at stake, but I think enough has been said already, indeed it would occupy more space in this work than can be spared to detail one half, even, of the annual amount of business transacted at this place. Besides occupying so important a position as a market centre, Chicago's growth and increasing prosperity as a manufacturing centre within the fifty years of its existence, is a fact almost equally marvellous. The manufacturing establishments of the Queen City have acquired a world-wide reputation, and their name is legion. There are iron foundries and brass foundries, marble works, brick yards (in 1879 Chicago turned out 40,000,000 bricks), silver-smelting works, silver-plating works, reaping-machine manufactories, sewing-machine manufactories, cotton mills and flour mills, tanneries and breweries and distilleries by the dozen. Each and all of these have done a "rushing" business during the past year; other industries, too numerous to mention have been prosperous likewise. The total value of Chicago's manufactures during the year 1879 amounted to 236,500,000 dollars: the total value of her entire trade of 1879 amounted to 764,000,000 dollars, a net gain of seventeen-and-a-half per cent. over her entire trade of 1878. Surely with this, and with such facts as we have above indicated, it may truly be said that this city, so young, so flourishing, possessing such vast interests, such grand resources, the great emporium of a new world springing up, as it were, into life, has a future before it such as no other city in the world can anticipate.

DOCUMENT NO. 17

A VISIT TO THE FORD FACTORY IN DETROIT*

Frank Dilnot, an English author, arrived in the United States early in 1917. The book resulting from his sojourn there is a commentary on a variety of American customs and attitudes. The exact date of his visit to Detroit is not known, but while there he toured the Ford factory, where he observed the operation of the assembly line that produced automobiles.

γ   γ   γ

It was the same afternoon that I went and saw another wonderful thing, namely the miracle known as Ford's factory. I regard it as one of the sights of the world. Here is an establishment which employs thirty-four thousand men, no man of whom after six months service receives less than five dollars a day—obtaining up to that time three dollars and fifty cents. Throughout the whole of the previous year only two men had been discharged because it is a rule of the factory that if a man is not suitable for one job he is put in some other position for which he is better adapted. I saw how the Ford motor car is manufactured. There is a bench, breast-high, winding its way through hundreds of yards of the factory, and along that bench at intervals of a yard on either side stand workmen. Above the bench within reach run forward-moving belts containing various parts of the motor car. The nucleus of the car, about the size of a bushel basket, is placed on the bench in front of the first of the men, and by means of a travelling carriage passes on a slow but continuous journey between the two lines. Each man does something to that nucleus, or adds something as it passes, and by the time it has traversed over the winding line it has been built up by the hundreds of workmen into practically a complete car. And these cars follow each other at intervals of seconds only.

---

* Frank Dilnot, *The New America, by an Englishman* (New York: Macmillan, 1919), 136–37.

DOCUMENT NO. 18

INDUSTRIAL PITTSBURGH*

A former American army officer and the author of a number of books, Captain Willard Glazier spent several years visiting many of the cities of the United States, and he published those observations in 1886. His description of industrial activity in Pittsburgh is fairly detailed, and the picture he paints is not always an attractive one.

γ   γ   γ

Pittsburg [*sic*] is situated in western Pennsylvania, in a narrow valley at the confluence of the Allegheny and Monongahela rivers, and at the head of the Ohio, and is surrounded by hills rising to the height of four or five hundred feet. These hills once possessed rounded outlines, with sufficient exceptional abruptness to lend them variety and picturesqueness. But they have been leveled down, cut into, sliced off, and ruthlessly marred and mutilated, until not a trace of their original outlines remain. Great black coal cars crawl up and down their sides, and plunge into unexpected and mysterious openings, their sudden disappearance lending, even in daylight, an air of mystery and diablerie to the region. Railroad tracks gridiron the ground everywhere, debris of all sorts lies in heaps, and is scattered over the earth, and huts and hovels are perched here and there, in every available spot. There is no verdure—nothing but mud and coal, the one yellow the other black. And on the edge of the city are the unpicturesque outlines of factories and foundries, their tall chimneys belching forth columns of inky blackness, which roll and whirl in fantastic shapes, and finally lose themselves in the general murkiness above.

The tranquil Monongahela comes up from the south, alive with barges and tug boats; while the swifter current of the Allegheny bears from the oil regions, at the north, slight-built barges with their freights of crude petroleum. Oil is not infrequently poured upon the troubled waters, when one of these barges sinks, and its freight, liberated from the open tanks, refuses to sink with it, and spreads itself out on the surface of the stream.

* Willard Glazier, *Peculiarities of American Cities* (Philadelphia: Hubbard Brothers, 1886), 335–42.

The oil fever was sorely felt in Pittsburg, and it was a form of malaria against which the smoke-laden atmosphere was no protection. During the early years of the great oil speculation the city was in a perpetual state of excitement. Men talked oil upon the streets, in the cars and counting-houses, and no doubt thought of oil in church. Wells and barrels of petroleum, and shares of oil stock were the things most often mentioned. And though that was nearly twenty years ago, and the oil speculation has settled into a safe and legitimate pursuit, Pittsburg is still the greatest oil mart in the world. By the means of Oil Creek and the Allegheny, the oil which is to supply all markets is first shipped to Pittsburg, passes through the refineries there, and is then exported.

The Ohio River makes its beginning here, and in all but the season of low water the wharves of the city are lined with boats, barges and tugs, destined for every mentionable point on the Ohio and Mississippi rivers. The Ohio River is here, as all along its course, an uncertain and capricious stream. Sometimes, in spring or early summer, it creeps up its banks and looks menacingly at the city. At other times it seems to become weary of bearing the boats, heavily laden with merchandise, to their destined ports, and so takes a nap, as it were. The last time we beheld this water-course its bed was lying nearly bare and dry, while a small, sluggish creek, a few feet, or at most a few yards wide, crept along the bottom, small barges being towed down stream by horses, which waded in the water. The giant was resting. . . .

The crowning glory of Pittsburg is her monster iron and glass works. One-half the glass produced in all the United States comes from Pittsburg. This important business was first established here in 1787, by Albert Gallatin, and it has increased since then to giant proportions. Probably, not less than one hundred millions of bottles and vials are annually produced here, besides large quantities of window glass. The best wine bottles in America are made here, though they are inferior to those of French manufacture. A great number of flint-glass works turn out the best flint glass produced in the country.

In addition to these glass works—which, though they employ thousands of workmen, represent but a fraction of the city's industries—there are rolling mills, foundries, potteries, oil refineries, and factories of machinery. All these works are rendered possible by the coal which abounds in measureless quantities in the immediate neighborhood of the city. All the hills which rise from the river back of Pittsburg have a thick stratum of bituminous coal running through them, which can be mined without shafts, or any of the usual accessories of mining. All that is to be done is to shovel the coal out of the hill-side, convey it in cars or by means of an inclined plane to the factory or foundry door, and dump it, ready for use. In fact, these hills are but immense coal cellars, ready filled for the convenience of the Pittsburg manufacturers. . . . Probably not less than ten thousand men are employed in these coal mines in and near Pittsburg, adding a population not far from fifty thousand to that region. Pittsburg herself consumes one-third of the coal produced, and a large proportion of the rest is shipped down the Ohio and Mississippi rivers, some of it as far as New Orleans.

The monster iron works of Pittsburg consume large quantities of this coal, and it is the abundance and convenience of the latter material which have made the former possible. No other city begins to compare with Pittsburg in the number and variety of her factories. Down by the banks of the swift-flowing Allegheny most of the great foundries are to be discovered. The Fort Pitt Works are on a gigantic scale. Here are cast those monsters of artillery known as the twenty-inch gun. . . .

The American Iron Works employ two thousand five hundred hands, and cover seventeen acres. They have a coal mine at their back door, and an iron mine on Lake Superior, and they make any and every difficult iron thing the country requires. Nothing is too ponderous, nothing too delicate and exact, to be produced. The nail works of the city are well worth seeing. In them a thousand nails a minute are manufactured, each nail being headed by a blow on cold iron. The noise arising from this work can only be described as deafening. In one nail factory two hundred different kinds of nails, tacks and brads are manufactured. The productions of these different factories and foundries amount in the aggregate to an almost incredible number and value, and embrace everything made of iron which can be used by man.

. . . Actual measurement shows that there are, in the limits of what is known as Pittsburg, nearly thirty-five miles of manufactories of iron, of steel, of cotton, and of brass alone, not mentioning manufactories of other materials. In a distance of thirty-five and one-half miles of streets, there are four hundred and seventy-eight manufactories of iron, steel, cotton, brass, oil, glass, copper and wood, occupying less than four hundred feet each; for a measurement of the ground shows that these factories are so contiguous in their positions upon the various streets of the city, that if placed in a continuous row, they would reach thirty-five miles, and each factory have less than the average front stated. This is "manufacturing Pittsburg." In four years the sale and consumption of pig iron alone was one-fourth the whole immense production of the United States; and through the Ohio and Mississippi rivers and their tributaries, its people control the shipment of goods, without breaking bulk, over twelve thousand miles of water transportation, and are thus enabled to deliver the products of their thrift in nearly four hundred counties in the territory of fifteen States. There is no city of its size in the country which has so large a banking capital as Pittsburg. The Bank of Pittsburg, it is said, is the only bank in the Union that never suspended specie payments.

DOCUMENT NO. 19

ABANDONED FARMS IN NEW ENGLAND*

William Dean Howells was one of America's most influential novelists and critics. In A Traveller from Altruria, *he comments on many aspects of America of his time through the device of having a visitor from a fictitious country visit the United States. Here, this traveler is being guided through rural New England.*

γ   γ   γ

There was not very much of the soil cultivated, for the chief crop was hay, with here and there a patch of potatoes or beans, and a few acres in sweet-corn. The houses of the natives, when they were for their use only, were no better than their turnouts; it was where the city boarder had found shelter that they were modern and pleasant. Now and then we came to a deserted homestead, and I tried to make the Altrurian understand how farming in New England had yielded to the competition of the immense agricultural operations of the West. "You know," I said, "that agriculture is really an operation out there, as much as coal-mining is in Pennsylvania, or finance in Wall Street; you have no idea of the vastness of the scale." Perhaps I swelled a little with pride in my celebration of the national prosperity, as it flowed from our Western farms of five and ten and twenty thousand acres; I could not very well

---

* William Dean Howells, *A Traveller from Altruria* (New York: Harper & Brothers, 1908), 92–93.

help putting on the pedal in these passages. Mrs. Makely listened almost as eagerly as the Altrurian, for, as a cultivated American woman, she was necessarily quite ignorant of her own country, geographically, politically, and historically. "The only people left in the hill country of New England," I concluded, "are those who are too old or too lazy to get away. Any young man of energy would be ashamed to stay, unless he wanted to keep a boarding-house or live on the city vacationists in summer. If he doesn't, he goes West and takes up some of the new land, and comes back in middle-life and buys a deserted farm to spend his summers on."

DOCUMENT NO. 20

THE EVILS OF BOSTON*

The Reverend Henry Morgan was a dynamic and unconventional clergyman, who styled himself the "Poor Man's Preacher." He set out to document the ways Boston had strayed from the Puritan "City on a Hill" to the sinful city of his day, by hiring investigators to uncover the city's vices. He urged the residents of rural New England to avoid moving to Boston, where they undoubtedly would meet with a sorrowful fate.

γ   γ   γ

Boston is a representative city of America. As goes Boston so go the rest. What is the moral? It is this: "Flee the great cities! Oh young man, happy in your country home, come not to the great city! Flee its temptations, its poverty, and its crimes. Bring not the Sarahs of your early love to the tents of the Abimelechs, or the palaces of the Pharaohs. Anchor not among the shoals and quicksands of city life." . . .

Once more I lift my voice and cry against the "sins of a great city." I adjure the young, "Be contented in your country homes." . . .

Follow me as I invoke the spirit of Asmodeus, lift the roofs of the houses, remove the walls and unveil Boston's mysteries. Here we dis-

---

* Henry Morgan, *Boston Inside Out! Sins of a Great City! A Story of Real Life*, Tenth Thousand, Revised and Enlarged (Boston: Shawmut Publishing Company, 1880), iii–vi, 100–1, 490–92.

cover the secret of her degeneracy. Let us peer into the curtained chamber, tread the hidden arcades where pleasure holds high carnival, and behold the altars burning with incense to the genius of vice and crime. Now is the hour sacred to the rites of Anatis, Bel and Jezebel. Two hundred gaming-tables click and rattle, breathing hope and despair at the cast of the die or turn of the card. Two thousand liquor saloons blaze on the cheek of night with seductive invitation.

Here is a street of fifty houses once occupied by respectable owners, now leased to doubtful occupants, all kept for lodgers, save two; and "*no questions asked!*" Three fourths of these lodgers are females, half of them having no visible occupation. One hundred women in one short street living in idleness and vice! Here Piper struck with the hammer his sleeping victim before murdering Mabel Young. Here Julia Hawkes was met by Costello and led out to be murdered. Here Jennie Clark met her seducer, and was led to the foul den from which she never returned. Here a gay bank cashier met the actress who caused his ruin. Through her he became a defaulter to the sum of $40,000. Here the nephew instigated by his mistress planned the robbery of his uncle's safe, obtaining $30,000. Here a Fast Young Man driven to desperation by fear of discovery, went out to take his life because he had embezzled $300 from his employers.

This street is notorious in the annals of crime. Yet Boston has many such streets. Here are miles on miles of lodging-houses instead of homes. Thousands of young men have only a private room, without a fire, destitute of all endearing charms. With no fond ties of affection; no wife, mother, sister, or child to make home dear; no sweet meal blessed by love's tender smiles. A solitary room, a lunch out, without a kind word or a friend to cheer, or a night in the street, in a saloon, at some cheap place of amusement or more doubtful resort; then returning to his cheerless chamber, to wait the coming of weary morn.

Such is clerk life, shop life, single life in Boston. No wonder people thus exposed yield to the temptations of false love, fall in the net, seek mediums and questionable affinities to soothe their lonely hours. . . .

O, Boston, Boston! Once the pride of all America! Beacon light of freedom! Shield of the exiled! Refuge of the oppressed! Home of culture! What shall be thy doom?

Boston is New England's headquarters of temptation. The monster mill that grinds and crushes innocent beings, gathered from every New

England State. The gigantic serpent that charms, envenoms, and consumes. Thousands of guileless and unsuspecting ones are fascinated and enticed from their country homes, and become food for the serpent's maw.

This food furnishes a virus that beats back in poisonous veins to every hill-top and home. . . . .

Maine and New Hampshire groan at every throb of Boston's wicked heart.

The contaminations of her poison, rum-shops, brothels, her gambling dens, her licentious amusements pulsate back to every city and town.

The pine woods of Maine whisper sighs over her lost children. Maine's struggle against strong drink is marvellous. She cries, "O greedy Boston, do not force the cup to our children''s lips!"

The granite hills of New Hampshire look down in grief and sorrow upon her desolate homes, robbed to fill Boston's dens of shame.

The waves of the Connecticut, the Merrimac, and Penobscot bear tears, sorrows, and wailings to the sea. The sea takes up the lamentations and pours them into Boston Harbor.

Ten thousand cyprians walk her streets. One thousand die every year. Placed hand to hand they extend a mile. One mile of human beings marching in funeral procession to the grave. Three hundred victims in the prison-house at Deer Island.

In sight of Deer Island is Nahant with its four millions of gold. Summer seat by the sea! Hark, a storm! The beetling crags beat back ocean's tempestuous charges and laugh at the wreck of waves breaking at their feet.

In those cells are three hundred victims who could not resist the waves of temptation. Instead of standing up like the rock, they bent their heads like the willow.

Solicitations of pampered libertines glittering in wealth were more potent than ocean waves.

Hark, some are dying! The cries of three hundred Deer Island cells echo their moanings to the sea.

Two great sewers pass down Boston Harbor. One empties to the sea. The other through Deer Island to eternity. One now in construction to Moon Island beneath the surface tunnelling the ocean. The other a great moral sewer of sin. Outlet of Boston's death streams.

DOCUMENT NO. 21

THE CITY AS A MENACE*

Josiah Strong was a Congregationalist minister from Ohio, who was a popular writer and lecturer. He was concerned about the deterioration of life in America's cities, and he saw the infusion of large numbers of immigrants from southern and eastern Europe as a significant factor contributing to this decline.

γ   γ   γ

What, then, is the prospect for the future? The fact that an ever-increasing proportion of population must live in the city is not reassuring as to moral growth. The decay of Italian agriculture and the migration of population to Rome accompanied and stimulated the decay of Roman morals. Mr. Lecky says: "It would be difficult to overrate the influence of agriculture in forming temperate and virtuous habits among the people." It will be much more difficult to maintain a high moral standard in a nation of cities than it would be among an agricultural people. . . . .

We are now prepared to weigh the gravity of the fact that more than one half of our population will soon be urban, and that in due time we shall be a nation of cities. If the rate of the movement of population from country to city, between 1890 and 1900 continues until 1940, there will then be in the United States 21,000,000 more people in our cities than outside of them. If the rate of growth above referred to is not sustained, it will make a difference of a few years only, as the preponderance of our city population in the near future must be regarded as certain. The cities will then no longer accept limitations from the state, but, when they have become fully conscious of their power, will take into their hands not only their own affairs, but also those of the state and of the nation. . . .

Most of our great cities have at some time been in the hands of a mob. In the summer of 1892, within a few days of each other, New York, Pennsylvania, and Tennessee ordered out their militia, and Idaho called

* Josiah Strong, *The Challenge of the City* (New York: American Baptist Home Mission Society, 1907), 52, 61–67.

on the United States Government for troops to suppress labor riots. More recent instances are not lacking. That is not self-government, but government by military force. There is peril when the Goddess of Liberty is compelled to lean on the point of a bayonet for support. Sooner or later it will pierce her hand.

The city, in a position to dictate to state and nation, and yet incapable of self-government, is like Nero on the throne. As the city by virtue of its preponderating population, is soon to ascend the throne, it is well to glance at some of the powers which are reaching after the city's scepter.

As the saloon sustains important relations to the law, it desires to control both those who make the laws and those whose duty it is to enforce them. It has already become a political institution of power. Politicians are careful not to antagonize it. . . .

The saloon is much stronger in the city than in the country; indeed, there are few cities in the United States which the liquor power is not able to dominate. What if the saloon controls the city when the city controls state and nation?

Again, another fact which must be faced is that our foreign population is largely concentrated in the city.

We do not forget our indebtedness to the immigrants. They have borne the brunt of the toil and hardship in subduing the continent and in developing its resources. They shared the sacrifice to save the Union. They have enriched the literature of every profession, and many are among our best citizens, intelligently and enthusiastically devoted to American institutions. Not a few of our truest Americans, as our Irish friends might say, were not born in their native land. They became Americans by choice, we only by accident. Oftentimes the patriotism of the naturalized citizen shames that of the native-born. Here is a vast amount of valuable raw material out of which admirable Americans can be made. Indeed, most of the races coming to us have desirable qualities in which we are deficient; and, if they fail to make valuable contributions to our civilization, we ourselves shall be primarily responsible. Whether the immigrants are to remain aliens or become Americans depends much more on us than on them.

But we must not be blind to the fact that in several ways the foreign population puts a great strain on our institutions. Many are naturalized without being Americanized, which means ignorant power; and that is always dangerous. The proportion of illiterates among our foreign-born population (12.9 per cent.) Is nearly three times as large as among the native whites (4.6 per cent.). In 1900 there were 65,008 native whites in the United States at least ten years of age, born of foreign parentage, who could not speak the English language.

Those who are foreign by birth or parentage, though constituting about one third of the population, furnish 6,000 more paupers supported in the alms-houses than the native white element, and nearly as many as the native whites and blacks together. That is, the tendency to pauperism in this country is nearly three times as strong in the foreign element as in the native.

Again, of the prisoners in the United States, omitting those whose parentage is unknown, the foreign element furnishes 56.81 per cent. In other words, the tendency to crime in the United States is more than two and one half times as strong among those who are foreign by birth or parentage, as among those who are native.

Juvenal complained that Syrian Orontes had flowed into the Tiber, and brought with it its language and morals. In like manner, our American waters have been fouled by many an Orontes of the Old World.

When we consider that the quality of immigration is growing less desirable, it is not reassuring to reflect that Europe could send us an unceasing stream of 3,000,000 every year—as many as our entire population in twenty-eight years or 300,000,000 in a century—and yet leave the present source of supply not only unimpaired but even increased; and until economic conditions have been equalized between Europe and America the stream will continue to flow.

Judging the future by the past, it is improbable that any legislation will dam this stream. Our population will continue to swell by this foreign flood, and whatever strain it puts on American institutions, that strain is more than three times as great in our large cities as in the whole country. In 1890, of the male population in our eighteen largest cities, 1,028,122 were native-born of native parentage, 1,386,776 were foreign-born, and 1,450,733 were native-born of foreign parentage; that is, those who were foreign by birth or parentage numbered 2,837,509, or more than two and a half times as many as the native American stock. This proportion has been largely increased by the immigration of the last sixteen years.

These elements, as they come to us, are clay in the hands of the political potter. If they remain uninstructed as to good citizenship, and incapable of forming individual judgments concerning public questions, the boss will certainly rule the city when the city rules the nation.

DOCUMENT NO. 22

POLISH MIGRANTS*

Included in William I. Thomas and Florian Znaniecki's landmark study, The Polish Peasant in Europe and America, *is a selection of letters written to the Emigrants Protective Association in Warsaw by prospective migrants to America, who hoped to obtain useful information. These documents are valuable for gaining an understanding of the reasons for migration.*

γ   γ   γ

1. I intend to go in a few days to a Jewish agent in Konstantynów to make an arrangement for crossing the frontier without a passport, for I am absolutely determined to go now to New York or Philadelphia to earn some hundreds of roubles there within 2 or 3 years and then to come back to our country and rent a mill or buy a piece of land with the money collected in this way.

Before going to the Jew I went to call on the priest in Butowce, who already knew from my wife's relatives that I had resolved to go to America. Well, at first he advised me not to leave my country; he showed me the dangers, the terrible work there which often costs one's life, and in general the reasons why it is not worth leaving here. But I was not persuaded. Then he advised me to write to you . . . and to wait for your answer. I obeyed and now I beg you to send me the necessary information. . . .

I am 26 years old, a Catholic, Polish and in perfect health. I was married about a year ago. I can read and write Polish and Russian. My specialty is gardening, but I know other handicrafts also—carpenter's, tailor's, shoemaker's and wheelwright's work. I left my place as gardener a week ago. I was paid there 120 roubles a year, with board, lodging, light and fuel. . . . .I have parents but do not live with them. I have neither land nor house of my own.

2. Praised by Jesus Christus. . . . I inform you that I intend to emigrate to America where I have many friends, for the most part relatives, who write that I can come to them and they will find work for me. . . . I know only one handicraft, carpenter's. I practiced with a country car-

* William I. Thomas and Florian Znaniecki, *The Polish Peasant in Europe and America*, 2 vols. (New York: Alfred A. Knopf, 1927), 2:1504–8.

penter, but at the present time it is very difficult to find material, and therefore difficult to earn.

We have little land, and I have a sister and two brothers. I am 18 years old; so if I can go to America and get work, as I have the intention of doing, before the call to the army I could earn still more money. . . . I know how to read and I read many books and papers. . . . I also know something about writing, as you can see from this letter. I have been to some monthly agricultural courses in Lublin, where I learned a little about the science of agriculture and model farming. . . . I hope if I live to try with all my strength to organize a model farm but now, because of lack of money and because my father has still a debt, it is difficult to make practical improvements in any way or to buy agricultural machincs, which are very dear.

4. Respected Gentlemen, Benefactors of Mankind! Having learned that in Warsaw there exists a society to assist those who emigrate abroad, and because I who write intend to emigrate from my country, I address myself to you, respected gentlemen, with the prayer and the confidence of a child [and ask] that you answer this question for me: "Where is now the best place for me, poor self-taught peasant (because everything I know, I learned from Reussner's Method, *i.e.*, to write Polish and Russian, a little German, and now I am learning English). Where can I employ best my good strength and health?"

I am now 28 years old, a bachelor. I have done my military service in the Russo-Japanese campaign. . . . I was set free with the grade of regimental clerk. Since I returned from the army, *i.e.*, 2908, I have worked as farm-clerk. But I have had no school instruction, no means, no favorable circumstances and no time for self-education. And moreover, I am of peasant extraction. All this together is the chief impediment in the way of my development and happiness. There is no place for me, poor man, in the government service—and I don't want it. I know no handicraft, for I learned none. Until my 21st year, *i.e.*, till my military service, I was with my parents in the country in the Kingdom [of Poland] where they own a piece of land. I helped them in their work and during the time I could spare I studied, for I had an unconquerable desire to read and write.

And thus, respected gentlemen, in the past as in the present some interior, insuperable force pushed me *forward* and ordered me to work and live economically—now also I live economically, drink very little and don't smoke at all—and to come back to my country only to set up an independent business for, as I have ascertained, *only self-reliant, independent work brings good fruits.*

I will await impatiently your answer, respected gentlemen, in which I beg you to indicate: 1) The land; 2) the nationality; 3) the language; 4) the kind of work; 5) the most suitable time for the journey; 6) the cost of the journey; 7) the indispensable clothes for the journey; 8) data about the documents for crossing [the frontier].

5. I have a very great wish to go to America. I want to leave my native country because we are 6 children and we have very little land, only about 6 morgs and some small farm-buildings, so that our whole farm is worth 1200 roubles at the highest. And my parents are still young; father is 48 and mother 42 years old. So it is difficult for us to live. Father got me married and gave me a dowry of 200 roubles, and I received 200 roubles with my wife. So father has given me my share and now I am alone with my wife. I have no children yet. Here in our country one must work plenty and wages are very small, just enough to live, so I would like to go in the name of our Lord God; perhaps I would earn more there. I will leave my wife with her father, *i.e.*, my father-in-law. I have 200 roubles for the journey. I am a healthy boy 24 years old. I do not fear any work.

8. I want to go to America, but I have no means at all because I am poor and have nothing but the ten fingers of my hands, a wife and 9 children. I have no work at all, although I am strong and healthy and only 45 years old. I cannot earn for my family. I have been already in Dombrowa, Sosnowiec, Zawiercie and Łódź, wherever I could go, and nowhere could I earn well. And here they [the children] call for food and clothing and more or less education. I wish to work, not easily only but even hard, but what can I do? I will not go to steal and I have no work.

So I beg the Protective Association to accept me for this journey and not only me, but I should like to take with me two of my children, a boy 16 and a girl 18 years old. And I beg the Association. There are still other people who would readily go to America. They are also poor.

9. I live in the district of Żytomierz. I have no land of my own. I am not a craftsman and it is very difficult for me to live here. I rent some *desiatinas* [a *desiatina* is about 2 acres] of land from an estate-owner. I have to pay 15 roubles rent for each desiatina. . . . And now I cannot pay the rent to the proprietor; therefore I must soon leave this place. But where can I find a piece of bread with a wife and two children? Because

of this difficulty, having no work, I address myself to the respected directors with the request that they advise and protect me in my journey to America. . . . I do not intend to go with my whole family because I have too little money. I am merely looking for work for some time.

DOCUMENT NO. 23

TENEMENTS OF NEW YORK*

Reports of the squalid living conditions endured by poor tenement house dwellers in New York City led the New York State Assembly to appoint a committee to investigate these dwellings in New York City and Brooklyn. That committee performed a thorough survey of the slums of those cities, and it issued its report in 1857. The following excerpt from that report details some of their findings.

γ γ γ

. . . At 97 Washington-street the committee visited an old building, three stories high, 18 by 30 feet in area, very much out of repair and extremely filthy. In a cellar beneath rooms were "to let." The first floor was used by the lessee as a sailors' lodging-house, the accommodation of which consisted of bunks, arranged one above another like a ship's lockers. The upper floors were occupied by Irish families, to the height of the garret, which was reached by a kind of ladder. Under the broken and leaky roof three families were crouching, one of which (a woman and child) paid three dollars per month for a portion of the miserable garret; the woman had been obliged to sell her bedstead to meet the rent, and slept with her baby on the floor. The total rent collected from tenants in this house (18 by 30 feet, and three stories) was $90 per month.

At 46 Trinity-place (third ward), in rear of Trinity church, and overlooked by the stained windows of that beautiful edifice, was a tenant-house, which had been altered from a school building; in this house there were fourteen families—in all seventy-six persons—each tenement comprising a room 12 by 14 feet in area, with two bed-rooms, or

---

* State of New York, *Report of the Select Committee Appointed to Examine into the Condition of Tenant Houses in New-York and Brooklyn* (Assembly Doc. 205, March 9, 1857), 16–19.

rather closets, where neither light nor air penetrated. Some of the families inhabiting these premises kept lodgers at one shilling per night. One widow woman had nine men boarding with her, dwelling in the one dining-room and two bed-rooms. In this range of tenements, rear of Trinity church, epidemics have originated on two distinct occasions— the yellow fever, several years since, and, more recently, the cholera. Filth and want of ventilation are enough to infect the very walls with disease.

At No. 51, Worth street, (fifth ward) the Committee inspected a building in the last stages of decay, though two or three wretched families still clung to it. The rear rooms of this ruin, even with the ground, appear to be abandoned to general filth and excrements. Such a nuisance must sicken a whole neighborhood with its noisomeness.

In Mulberry street, near the "Five Points," (sixth ward,) the Committee examined a large tenant house, in a very dilapidated condition. It had been reconstructed, through its interior, from an old wooden church, once used by the Baptists, and adapted to occupancy in the most careless manner. The sewer connection, serving for the premises, was a four inch pipe, wholly inadequate to the necessary uses of such a conduit. In this establishment there were 85 apartments, containing more than 100 families, and comprising 310 persons. In the basement, entered by shattered steps, the depth below the street level was measured by the committee, and ascertained to be five feet, two inches. In these vaults, families were dwelling, and paying $3 per month, for their damp and sickly quarters. On the fifth floor of this structure $4.50 per month was paid for apartments. The entire fabric is cased and partitioned with pine boards, its entries and passages dark and cramped, and the walls, floors and roofing of such inflammable materials that, in case of fire in any portion, it would be impossible to arrest its spread. Should such a calamity take place at night, it is more than probable that scores of the unfortunate inmates would perish ere they could find egress through the narrow doors and passages. Yet, in this building, bad as it is, the main entrances are wider than in most of the re-constructed, or even specially-built tenant-houses, one of the latter of which has been erected on the front lots.

At No. 17 Baxter-street, the Committee penetrated through an alley-passage, where the black mud was two inches deep, to a rear entrance under the building; the basement rooms, with floor five and a half feet below the street-level, was occupied as a dance-house and bar-room, the former 27 feet by 16, the latter 13 by 16, for which $13 per month was paid; two beds for lodgers were in the dance-room. The class of basement or cellar lodgers accommodated in such places pay from six-pence to a shilling per night; average number of lodgers to one bed is three, and no distinction is made between male and female. On the upper floors of this tenant-house, twelve families, comprising seventy-five persons, dwelt in twelve apartments; walls damp, rooms dark, passages filthy, and with no sort of ventilation. Rear of these premises was a collection of sheds built of rough boards, each containing four dark rooms, rent $3 per month, inhabited by poor people who subsisted by the sale of spearmint, which they grew in boxes on the roof, and disposed of to hotels and bar-rooms, a fact which suggested that certain fashionable beverages in vogue might be traced back for their constituents to the malaria and filth of the Five Point tenant-houses. The average rent of rooms in this locality, where are many houses of the same description, is $4 per month.

At the rear of 37½ Baxter-street (ground said to be the lowest in the city) apartments were entered six feet beneath the street level, ceilings barely six feet in height, renting at $4 per month, and on the second story of the house a rear room, with two dark closets, rented for $5 per month, and a front room at $6.50, the latter to a family consisting of an old dame of sixty and two daughters, who supported themselves by picking curled hair sixteen hours per day, the three earning five dollars per week.

At 39 Baxter-street, a rear building, the Committee found fifteen persons living in one room, the height of which, from floor to ceiling, was seven feet, and the floor 15 feet by 14, rent $6 per month. To reach these premises it was necessary to pass through an alley, the widest portion of which was but two feet, the narrowest nineteen inches. In case of fires escape to the street would be a miracle. In the vicinity of this habitation were many other forlorn and squalid houses, let in the same way, at the average price of $7 per month.

REMARKS ON THESE HOUSES.

In this connection it may be mentioned that rear buildings and their surroundings, present, in general, the most repulsive features of the tenant-house system. As business has increased upon the streets, the buildings located favorably for stores have been converted to the use of trade, and the area comprised in the distance intervening, from square to square, generally filled with wooden structures, has been seized upon by the tenant-house speculator. Sometimes a dozen narrow and dark apartments in a single house, but often a collection of mouldy walls, covering a space of from forty to two hundred feet square, with cramped, miserable apartments, scarce fit for dog kennels, may be discovered in the rear of some busy factory in our lower wards, or seen from the windows of a hotel, or overlooked from the roof of a marble store. To reach these tumbling and squalid rookeries, the visitor must sometimes penetrate a labyrinth of alleys, behind horse stables, blacksmith's forges, and, inevitably, beside cheap groggeries, till he finds himself in a dim close, thick with mephitic gases, and nauseous from the effluvia of decaying matter and pools of stagnant water. . . .

DOCUMENT NO. 24

NEW YORK'S 1867 TENEMENT HOUSE ACT*

In 1867 the nation's first act regulating housing went into effect. This precedent-setting legislation did little to relieve the misery of the many thousands of tenement house occupants in New York and Brooklyn, but it was at least a first step. A reading of the provisions of this act make clear how horrible living conditions were in the slums, and how unacceptable they would have been even if all its provisions were enforced.

γ   γ   γ

SECTION 1. From and after the first day of July, eighteen hundred and sixty-seven, no house, building, or portion thereof, in the cities of New York or Brooklyn, shall be used, occupied, leased or rented for a tenement or lodging-house unless the same conforms in its construction and appurtenances to the requirements of this act.

§ 2. Every house, building or portion thereof, in the cities of New York and Brooklyn, designed to be used, occupied, leased or rented, or which is used, occupied, leased or rented for a tenement or lodging-house, shall have in every room which is occupied as a sleeping room,

---

* *New York State Laws*, Nineteenth Session, 1867, Chap. 908, 2265–72.

and which does not communicate directly with the external air, a ventilating or transom window, having an opening or area of three square
feet, over the door leading into and connected with the adjoining room,
if such adjoining room communicates with the external air, and also a
ventilating or transom window of the same opening or area, communicating with the entry or hall of the house, or where this is, from the
relative situation of the rooms impracticable, such last mentioned ventilating or transom window shall communicate with an adjoining room
that itself communicates with an adjoining room that itself communicates with the entry or hall. Every such house or building shall have in
the roof, at the top of the hall, an adequate and proper ventilator, of a
form approved in New York by the inspector of public buildings, and in
Brooklyn by the assistant sanitary superintendent of the Metropolitan
board of health.

§ 3. Every such house shall be provided with a proper fire escape, or
means of escape in case of fire, to be approved in New York by the inspector of public buildings, and in Brooklyn by the assistant sanitary
superintendent of the Metropolitan board of health.

§ 4. The roof of every such house shall be kept in good repair, and so
as not to leak, and all rain water shall be so drained or conveyed therefrom as to prevent its dripping on to the ground, or causing dampness
in the walls, yard or area. All stairs shall be provided with proper ban-
isters or railings, and shall be kept in good repair.

§ 5. Every such building shall be provided with good and sufficient
water-closets or privies, of a construction approved by the Metropolitan
board of health, and shall have proper doors, traps, soil pans, and other
suitable works and arrangements, so far as may be necessary to insure
the efficient operation thereof. Such water-closets or privies shall not be
less in number than one to every twenty occupants of said house; but
water-closets or privies may be used in common by the occupants of any
two or more houses, provided the access is convenient and direct, and
provided the number of occupants in the houses for which they are provided shall not exceed the proportion above required for every privy or
water-closet. Every such house situated upon a lot on a street in which
there is a sewer, shall have the water-closets or privies furnished with a
proper connection with the sewer, which connection shall be in alll its
parts adequate for the purpose, so as to permit entirely and freely to
pass whatever enters the same. Such connection with the sewer shall be

of a form approved in New York by the Croton aqueduct board, and in Brooklyn by the board of water commissioners. All such water-closets and vaults shall be provided with the proper traps, and connect with the house sewer by a proper tight pipe, and shall be provided with sufficient water and other proper means of flushing the same; and every owner, lessee and occupant shall take adequate measures to prevent improper substances from entering such water-closets or privies or their connections, and to secure the prompt removal of any improper substances that may enter them, so that no accumulation shall take place, and so as to prevent any exhalations therefrom, offensive, dangerous or prejudicial to life or health, and so as to prevent the same from being or becoming obstructed. No cess-pool shall be allowed in or under or connected with any such house, except when it is unavoidable, and in such case it shall be constructed in such situation and in such manner as the Metropolitan board of health may direct. It shall in all cases be water-tight, and arched or securely covered over, and no offensive smell or gases shall be allowed to escape therefrom, or from any privy or privy vault. In all cases where a sewer exists in the street upon which the house or building stands, the yard or area shall be so connected with the same that all water, from the roof or otherwise, and all liquid filth shall pass freely into it. Where no sewer exists in the street, the yard or area shall be so graded that all water, from the roof or otherwise, and all filth shall flow freely from it and all parts of it into the street gutter, by a passage beneath the sidewalk, which shall be covered by a permanent cover, but so arranged as to permit access to remove obstructions or impurities.

§ 6. From and after the first day of July, eighteen hundred and sixty-seven, it shall not be lawful, without a permit from the Metropolitan board of health, to let or occupy, or suffer to be occupied separately as a dwelling, any vault, cellar, or underground room built or rebuilt after said date, or which shall not have been so let or occupied before said date. And from and after July first, eighteen hundred and sixty-seven, it shall not be lawful without such permit to let or continue to be let, or to occupy or suffer to be occupied separately as a dwelling any vault, cellar or underground room whatsoever, unless the same be in every part thereof at least seven feet in height, measured from the floor to the ceiling thereof, nor unless the same be for at least one foot of its height above the surface of the street or ground adjoining or nearest to the same, nor unless there be outside of and adjoining the said vault, cellar or room, and extending along the entire frontage thereof, and upwards from six inches below the level of the floor thereof up to the surface of the said street or ground an open space of at least two feet and six inches wide in every part, nor unless the same be well and effectually drained by means of a drain, the uppermost part of which is one foot at least below the level of the floor of such vault, cellar or room, nor unless there is a clear space of not less than one foot below the level of the floor, except where the same is cemented, nor unless there be appurtenant to such vault, cellar or room the use of a water-closet or privy kept and provided as in this act required, nor unless the same have an external window opening of a least nine superficial feet clear of the sash frame, in which window opening there shall be fitted a frame filled in with glazed sashes, at least four and a half superficial feet of which shall be made so as to open for the purpose of ventilation. Provided, however, that in the case of an inner or back vault, cellar or room let or occupied along with a front vault, cellar or room, as part of the same letting or occupation. It shall be a sufficient compliance with the provisions of this act if the front room is provided with a window as hereinbefore pro- vided, and if the said back vault, cellar or room is connected with the front vault, cellar or room by a door and also by a proper ventilating or transom window, and where practicable also, connected by a proper ven- tilating or transom window, or by some hall or passage communicating with the external air. Provided always that in any area adjoining a vault, cellar or underground room there may be steps necessary for access to such vault, cellar or room, if the same be so placed as not to be over, across or opposite to the said external window, and so as to allow be- tween every part of such steps and the external wall of such vault, cellar or room, a clear space of six inches at least, and if the rise of said steps is open; and provided further that over or across any such area there may be steps necessary for access to any building above the vault, cellar or room to which such area adjoins, if the same be so placed as not to be over, across or opposite to any such external window.

§ 7. From and after the first day of July, eighteen hundred and sixty- eight, no vault, cellar or underground room shall be occupied as a place of lodging or sleeping, except the same shall be approved, in writing, and a permit given therefor by the Metropolitan board of health.

§ 8. Every tenement or lodging-house shall have the proper and suit- able conveniences or receptacles for receiving garbage and other refuse matters. No tenement or lodging-house, nor any portion thereof, shall be used as a place of storage for any combustible article, or any article dangerous to life or detrimental to health; nor shall any horse, cow, calf, swine, pig, sheep or goat be kept in said house. . . .

§ 13. It shall not be lawful hereafter to erect for, or convert to, the purposes of a tenement or lodging-house a building on the front of any lot where there is another building on the rear of the same lot, unless there is a clear open space exclusively belonging thereto, and extending upwards from the ground of at least ten feet between said buildings, if they are one story high above the level of the ground; if they are two stories high, the distance between them shall be not less than fifteen feet; if they are three stories high, the distance between them shall be twenty feet; and if they are more than three stories high, the distance between them shall be twenty-five feet. At the rear of every building hereafter erected for, or converted to the purposes of a tenement or lodging-house on back part of any lot, there shall be a clear, open space of ten feet between it and any other building. But when thorough ventilation of such open spaces can be otherwise secured, said distances may be lessened or modified, in special cases, by a permit from the Metropolitan board of health.

§ 14. In every such house hereafter erected or converted, every habitable room, except rooms in the attic, shall be in every part no less than eight feet in height from the floor to the ceiling; and every habitable room in the attic of any such building, shall be at least eight feet in height from the floor to the ceiling, throughout not less than one-half the area of such room. Every such room shall have, at least, one window, connecting with the external air, or over the door a ventilator of perfect construction, connecting it with a room or hall which has a connection with the external air, and so arranged as to produce a cross current of air. The total area of window or windows in every room communicating with the external air, shall be a least one-tenth of the superficial area of every such room; and the top of one, at least, of such windows, shall not be less than seven feet and six inches above te floor, and the upper half, at least, shall be made so as to open the full width. Every habitable room of a less area than one hundred superficial feet, if it does not communicate directly with the external air, and is without an open fireplace, shall be provided with special means of ventilation by a separate air shaft extending to the roof, or otherwise, as the board of health may prescribe. . . .

DOCUMENT NO. 25

MACHINE POLITICS IN NEW YORK*

George Washington Plunkitt, a late-nineteenth- and early-twentieth-century politician, served as a district leader for New York's Tammany Hall, and had held office as a New York State Senator. William L. Riordan, a reporter for the New York Evening Post, *set down Plunkitt's views on practical politics in a series of newspaper articles, which were published as a book in 1905. Plunkitt captured the essence of the way Tammany Hall operated, and his comments are a classic narrative on how to succeed in ward politics. Two of his most important musings are reproduced here.*

γ   γ   γ

Honest Graft and Dishonest Graft

Everybody is talkin' these days about Tammany men growin' rich on graft, but nobody thinks of drawin' the distinction between honest graft and dishonest graft. There's all the difference in the world between the two. Yes, many of our men have grown rich in politics. I have myself. I've made a big fortune out of the game, and I'm gettin' richer every day, but I've not gone in for dishonest graft—blackmailin' gamblers, saloonkeepers, disorderly people, etc.—and neither has any of the men who have made big fortunes in politics.

There's an honest graft, and I'm an example of how it works. I might sum up the whole thing by sayin': "I seen my opportunities and I took 'em."

Just let me explain by examples. My party's in power in the city, and it's goin' to undertake a lot of public improvements. Well, I'm tipped off, say, that they're going to lay out a new park at a certain place.

I see my opportunity and I take it. I go to that place and I buy up all the land I can in the neighborhood. Then the board of this or that makes its plan public, and there is a rush to get my land, which nobody cared particular for before.

Ain't it perfectly honest to charge a good price and make a profit on my investment and foresight? Of course, it is. Well, that's honest graft.

---

* William L. Riordon, *Plunkitt of Tammany Hall* (New York: McClure, Phillips, 1905), 3–10, 46–53.

Or supposin' it's a new bridge they're goin' to build. I get tipped off and I buy as much property as I can that has to be taken for approaches. I sell at my own price later on and drop some more money in the bank.

Wouldn't you? It's just like lookin' ahead in Wall Street or in the coffee or cotton market. It's honest graft, and I'm lookin' for it every day in the year. I will tell you frankly that I've got a good lot of it, too.

I'll tell you of one case. They were goin' to fix up a big park, no matter where. I got on to it, and went lookin' about for land in that neighborhood.

I could get nothin' at a bargain but a big piece of swamp, but I took it fast enough and held on to it. What turned out was just what I counted on. They couldn't make the park complete without Plunkitt's swamp, and they had to pay a good price for it. Anything dishonest in that?

Up in the watershed I made some money, too. I bought up several bits of land there some years ago and made a pretty good guess that they would be bought up for water purposes later by the city.

Somehow, I always guessed about right, and shouldn't I enjoy the profit of my foresight? It was rather amusin' when the condemnation commissioners came along and found piece after piece of the land in the name of George Plunkitt of the Fifteenth Assembly District, New York City. They wondered how I knew just what to buy. The answer is—I seen my opportunity and I took it. I haven't confined myself to land; anything that pays is in my line.

For instance, the city is repavin' a street and has several hundred thousand old granite blocks to sell. I am on hand to buy, and I know just what they are worth.

How? Never mind that. I had a sort of monopoly of this business for a while, but once a newspaper tried to do me. It got some outside men to come over from Brooklyn and New Jersey to bid against me.

Was I done? Not much. I went to each of the men and said: "How many of these 250,000 stones do you want?" One said 20,000, and another wanted 15,000, and another wanted 10,000. I said: "All right, let me bid for he lot, and I'll give each of you all you want for nothin'."

They agreed, of course. Then the auctioneer yelled: "How much am I bid for these 250,000 fine pavin' stones?"

"Two dollars and fifty cents," says I.

"Two dollars and fifty cents!" screamed the auctioneer. "Oh, that's a joke! Give me a real bid."

He found the bid was real enough. My rivals stood silent. I got the lot for $2.50 and gave them their share. That's how the attempt to do Plunkitt ended, and that's how all such attempts end.

I've told you how I got rich by honest graft. Now, let me tell you that most politicians who are accused of robbin' the city get rich the same way.

They didn't steal a dollar from the city treasury. They just seen their opportunities and took them. That is why, when a reform administration comes in and spends a half million dollars in tryin' to find the public robberies they talked about in the campaign, they don't find them.

The books are always all right. The money in the city treasury is all right. Everything is all right. All they can show is that the Tammany heads of departments looked after their friends, within the law, and gave them what opportunities they could to make honest graft. Now, let me tell you that's never goin' to hurt Tammany with the people. Every good man looks after his friends, and any man who doesn't isn't likely to be popular. If I have a good thing to hand out in private life, I give it to a friend. Why shouldn't I do the same in public life?

Another kind of honest graft. Tammany has raised a good many salaries. There was an awful howl by the reformers, but don't you know that Tammany gains ten votes for every one it lost by salary raisin'?

The Wall Street banker thinks it shameful to raise a department clerk's salary from $1500 to $1800 a year, but every man who draws a salary himself says: "That's all right. I wish it was me." And he feels very much like votin' the Tammany ticket on election day, just out of sympathy.

Tammany was beat in 1901 because the people were deceived into believin' that it worked dishonest graft. They didn't draw a distinction between dishonest and honest graft, but they saw that some Tammany men grew rich, and supposed they had been robbin' the city treasury or levyin' blackmail on disorderly houses, or workin' in with the gamblers and lawbreakers.

As a matter of policy, if nothing else, why should the Tammany leaders go into such dirty business, when there is so much honest graft lyin' around when they are in power? Did you ever consider that?

Now, in conclusion, I want to say that I don't own a dishonest dollar. If my worst enemy was given the job of writin' my epitaph when I'm gone, he couldn't do more than write:

"George W. Plunkitt. He Seen His Opportunities, and He Took 'Em."

To Hold Your District: Study Human Nature and Act Accordin'

There's only one way to hold a district: you must study human nature and act accordin'. You can't study human nature in books. Books is a hindrance more than anything else. If you have been to college, so much the worse for you. You'll have to unlearn all you learned before you can get right down to human nature, and unlearnin' takes a lot of time. Some men can never forget what they learned at college. Such men may get to be district leaders by a fluke, but they never last.

To learn real human nature you have to go among the people, see them and be seen. I know every man, woman, and child in the Fifteenth District, except them that's been born this summer—and I know some of them, too. I know what they like and what they don't like, what they are strong at and what they are weak in, and I reach them by approachin' at the right side.

For instance, here's how I gather in the young men. I hear of a young feller that's proud of his voice, thinks that he can sing fine. I ask him to come around to Washington Hall and join our Glee Club. He comes and sings, and he's a follower of Plunkitt for life. Another young feller gains a reputation as a baseball player in a vacant lot. I bring him into our baseball club. That fixes him. You'll find him workin' for my ticket at the polls next election day. Then there's the feller that likes rowin' on the river, the young feller that makes a name as a waltzer on his block, the young feller that's handy with his dukes—I rope them all in by givin' them opportunities to show themselves off. I don't trouble them with political arguments. I just study human nature and act accordin'.

But you may say this game won't work with the high-toned fellers, the fellers that go through college and then join the Citizens' Union. Of course it wouldn't work. I have a special treatment for them. I ain't like the patent medicine man that gives the same medicine for all diseases. The Citizens' Union kind of a young man! I love him! He's the daintiest morsel of the lot, and he don't often escape me.

Before telling you how I catch him, let me mention that before the election last year, the Citizens' Union said they had four hundred or five hundred enrolled voters in my district. They had a lovely headquarters too, beautiful roll-top desks and the cutest rugs in the world. If I was accused of havin' contributed to fix up the nest for them, I wouldn't deny it under oath. What do I mean by that? Never mind. You can guess from the sequel, if you're sharp.

Well, election day came. The citizens' Union's candidate for Senator, who ran against me, just polled five votes in the district, while I polled something more than 14,000 votes. What became of the 400 or 500 citizens' Union enrolled voters in my district? Some people guessed that many of them were good Plunkitt men all along and worked with the Cits just to bring them into the Plunkitt camp by election day. You can guess that way, too, if you want to. I never contradict stories about me, especially in hot weather. I just call your attention to the fact that on last election day 395 Citizens' Union enrolled voters in my district were missin' and unaccounted for.

I tell you frankly, though, how I have captured some of the Citizens' Union's young men. I have a plan that never fails. I watch the City Record to see when there's civil service examinations for good things. Then I take my young Cit in hand, tell him all about the good thing and get him worked up till he goes and takes an examination. I don't bother about him any more. It's a cinch that he comes back to me in a few days and asks to join Tammany Hall. Come over to Washington Hall some night and I'll show you a list of names on our rolls marked "C.S." which means, "bucked up against civil service."

As to the older voters, I reach them, too. No, I don't send them campaign literature. That's rot. People can get all the political stuff they want to read—and a good deal more, too—in the papers. Who reads speeches, nowadays, anyhow? It's bad enough to listen to them. You ain't goin' to gain any votes by stuffin' the letter boxes with campaign documents. Like as not you'll lose votes, for there's nothin' a man hates more than to hear the letter carrier ring his bell and go to the letter box expectin' to find a letter he was lookin' for, and find only a lot of printed politics. I met a man this very mornin' who told me he voted the Democratic State ticket last year just because the Republicans kept crammin' his letter box with campaign documents.

What tells in holdin' your grip on your district is to go right down among the poor families and help them in the different ways they need help. I've got a regular system for this. If there's a fire in Ninth, Tenth, or Eleventh Avenue, for example, any hour of the day or night, I'm usually there with some of my election district captains as soon as the fire engines. If a family is burned out I don't ask whether they are Republicans or Democrats, and I don't refer them to the Charity Organization Society, which would investigate their case in a month or two and decide they were worthy of help about the time they are dead from starvation.

I just get quarters for them, buy clothes for them if their clothes were burned up, and fix them up till they get things runnin' again. It's philanthropy, but it's politics, too—mighty good politics. Who can tell how many votes one of these fires bring me? The poor are the most grateful people in the world, and, let me tell you, they have more friends in their neighborhoods than the rich have in theirs.

If there's a family in my district in want I know it before the charitable societies do, and me and my men are first on the ground. I have a special corps to look up such cases. The consequence is that the poor look up to George W. Plunkitt as a father, come to him in trouble—and don't forget him on election day.

Another thing, I can always get a job for a deservin' man. I make it a point to keep on the track of jobs, and it seldom happens that I don't have a few up my sleeve ready for use. I know every big employer in the district and in the whole city, for that matter, and they ain't in the habit of sayin' no to me when I ask them for a job.

And the children—the little roses of the district! Do I forget them? Oh, no! They know me, every one of them, and they know that a sight of Uncle George and candy means the same thing. Some of them are the best kind of vote-getters. I'll tell you a case. Last year a little Eleventh Avenue rosebud, whose father is a Republican, caught hold of his whiskers on election day and said she wouldn't let go till he'd promise to vote for me. And she didn't.

BIBLIOGRAPHY

Allswang, John M. *Bosses, Machines, and Urban Voters*. Baltimore: Johns Hopkins University Press, 1986.

Anbinder, Tyler. *Five Points: The 19th-Century New York City Neighborhood That Invented Tap Dance, Stole Elections, and Became the World's Most Notorious Slum*. New York: The Free Press, 2001.

Barth, Gunther. *City People: The Rise of Modern City Culture in Nineteenth-Century America*. New York: Oxford University Press, 1980.

Bayor, Ronald H., and Timothy J. Meagher, eds. *The New York Irish*. Baltimore: Johns Hopkins University Press, 1996.

Blumin, Stuart M. *The Emergence of the Middle Class: Social Experience in the American City, 1760–1900*. New York: Cambridge University Press, 1989.

Bridenbaugh, Carl. *Cities in Revolt: Urban Life in America, 1743–1776*. New York: Capricorn, 1955.

——. *Cities in the Wilderness: The First Century of Urban Life in America, 1625–1742*. New York: Ronald Press, 1938.

Buenker, John D. *Urban Liberalism and Progressive Reform*. New York: Charles Scribner's Sons, 1973.

Burrows, Edwin G., and Mike Wallace. *Gotham: A History of New York City to 1898*. New York: Oxford University Press, 1999.

Callow, Alexander B. *The Tweed Ring*. New York: Oxford University Press, 1966.

Conzen, Kathleen Neils. *Immigrant Milwaukee, 1836–1860: Accommodation and Community in a Frontier City*. Cambridge, MA: Harvard University Press, 1976.

Cook, Adrian. *The Armies of the Streets: The New York City Draft Riots of 1863*. Lexington: University Press of Kentucky, 1974.

Cronon, William. *Nature's Metropolis: Chicago and the Great West*. New York: W. W. Norton, 1991.

Curry, Leonard P. *The Free Black in Urban America, 1800–1850: The Shadow of the Dream*. Chicago: University of Chicago Press, 1981.

Davis, Allen F. *Spearheads for Reform: The Social Settlements and the Progressive Movement, 1880–1914*. New York: Oxford University Press, 1967.

Doyle, Don H. *New Men, New Cities, New South: Atlanta, Nashville, Charleston, Mobile, 1860–1910*. Chapel Hill: University of North Carolina Press, 1989.

Dykstra, Robert R. *The Cattle Towns*. New York: Alfred A. Knopf, 1968.

Fogelson, Robert M. *The Fragmented Metropolis: Los Angeles, 1850–1930*. Cambridge, MA: Harvard University Press, 1967.

Fox, Kenneth. *Better City Government: Innovation in American Urban Politics, 1850–1937*. Philadelphia: Temple University Press, 1977.

Hammack, David C. *Power and Society: Greater New York at the Turn of the Century*. New York: Russell Sage Foundation, 1982.

Handlin, Oscar. *Boston's Immigrants: A Study in Acculturation*. Cambridge, MA: Harvard University Press, 1959.

Holli, Melvin G. *Reform in Detroit: Hazen S. Pingree and Urban Politics*. New York: Oxford University Press, 1969.

Hood, Clifton. *722 Miles: The Building of the Subways and How They Transformed New York*. New York: Simon & Schuster, 1994.

Howe, Irving. *World of Our Fathers: The Journey of the East European Jews to America and the Life They Found and Made*. New York: Harcourt Brace Jovanovich, 1976.

Johnson, David R. *Policing the Urban Underworld: the Impact of Crime on the Development of the American Police, 1800–1887*. Philadelphia: Temple University Press, 1979.

Kahn, Judd. *Imperial San Francisco: Politics and Planning in an American City, 1897–1906*. Lincoln: University of Nebraska Press, 1979.

Katzman, David M. *Before the Ghetto: Black Detroit in the Nineteenth Century*. Urbana: University of Illinois Press, 1973.

Kessner, Thomas. *The Golden Door: Italian and Jewish Immigrant Mobility in New York City, 1880–1915*. New York: Oxford University Press, 1977.

Lane, Roger. *Violent Death in the City: Suicide, Accident and Murder in Nineteenth-Century Philadelphia*. Cambridge, MA: Harvard University, 1979.

Leavitt, Judith Walzer. *The Healthiest City: Milwaukee and the Politics of Health Reform*. Princeton, NJ: Princeton University Press, 1982.

Lotchin, Roger W. *San Francisco, 1846–1856: From Hamlet to City*. New York: Oxford University Press, 1974.

McShane, Clay. *Technology and Reform: Street Railways and the Growth of Milwaukee, 1887–1900*. Madison: State Historical Society of Wisconsin, 1974.

Melosi, Martin V. *Garbage in the Cities: Refuse, Reform, and the Environment, 1880–1980*. Chicago: The Dorsey Press, 1981.

———., ed. *Pollution and Reform in American Cities, 1870–1930*. Austin: University of Texas Press, 1980.

Miller, Donald L. *City of the Century: The Epic of Chicago and the Making of America*. New York: Simon & Schuster, 1996.

Miller, Zane L. *Boss Cox's Cincinnati: Urban Politics in the Progressive Era*. New York: Oxford University Press, 1968.

Mohl, Raymond A. *The New City: Urban America in the Industrial Age, 1860–1920*. Wheeling, IL: Harlan Davidson, 1985.

Mormino, Gary Ross. *Immigrants on the Hill: Italian-Americans in St. Louis, 1882–1982*. Urbana: University of Illinois Press, 1986.

Nasaw, David. *Children of the City: At Work and At Play*. New York: Oxford University Press, 1986.

Nash, Gary. *The Urban Crucible: Social Change, Political Consciousness, and the Origins of the American Revolution.* Cambridge, MA: Harvard University Press, 1979.

Nelli, Humbert S. *The Italians in Chicago, 1860–1920: A Study in Ethnic Mobility.* New York: Oxford University Press, 1970.

O'Connor, Thomas H. *The Boston Irish: A Political History.* Boston: Northeastern University Press, 1995.

Peiss, Kathy. *Cheap Amusements: Working Women and Leisure in Turn-of-the-Century New York.* Philadelphia: Temple University Press, 1986.

Rabinowitz, Howard N. *Race Relations in the Urban South, 1865–1890.* New York: Oxford University Press, 1978.

Reps, John W. *The Making of Urban America: A History of City Planning in the United States.* Princeton, NJ: Princeton University Press, 1965.

Revell, Keith D. *Building Gotham: Civic Culture and Public Policy in New York City, 1898–1938.* Baltimore: Johns Hopkins University Press, 2003.

Rice, Bradley R. *Progressive Cities: the Commission Government Movement in America, 1901–1920.* Austin: University of Texas Press, 1977.

Richardson, James F. *Urban Police in the United States.* Port Washington, NY: Kennikat Press, 1974.

Riess, Steven A. *City Games: The Evolution of American Urban Society and the Rise of Sports.* Urbana, IL: University of Illinois Press, 1991.

Rosenberg, Charles E. *The Cholera Years: The United States in 1832, 1849, and 1866.* Chicago: University of Chicago Press, 1962.

Rosenzweig, Roy, and Elizabeth Blackmar. *The Park and the People: A History of Central Park.* Ithaca, NY: Cornell University Press, 1992.

Scheiner, Seth M. *Negro Mecca: A History of the Negro in New York City, 1865–1920.* New York: New York University Press, 1965.

Schiesl, Martin J. *The Politics of Efficiency: Municipal Administration and Reform in America: 1880–1920.* Berkeley: University of California Press, 1977.

Schuyler, David. *The New Urban Landscape: The Redefinition of City Form in Nineteenth-Century America.* Baltimore: Johns Hopkins University Press, 1986.

Shand-Tucci, Douglass. *Built in Boston: City and Suburb, 1800–1950.* Amherst: University of Massachusetts Press, 1988.

Shorto, Russell. *The Island at the Center of the World: The Epic Story of Dutch Manhattan and the Forgotten Colony That Shaped America.* New York: Doubleday, 2004.

Spann, Edward K. *The New Metropolis: New York City, 1840–1857.* New York: Columbia University Press, 1981.

Spear, Allan. *Black Chicago: The Making of a Negro Ghetto, 1890–1920.* Chicago: University of Chicago Press, 1967.

Srebnick, Amy Gilman. *The Mysterious Death of Mary Rogers: Sex and Culture in Nineteenth-Century New York*. New York: Oxford University Press, 1995.

Stansell, Christine. *City of Women: Sex and Class in New York, 1789–1860*. New York: Alfred A. Knopf, 1986.

Tarr, Joel A. *Transportation Innovation and Changing Spatial Patterns: Pittsburgh, 1850–1910*. Pittsburgh: Carnegie Mellon University, 1972.

Teaford, Jon C. *The Municipal Revolution in America: Origins of Modern Urban Government, 1650–1825*. Chicago: University of Chicago Press, 1975.

———. *The Unheralded Triumph: City Government in America, 1870–1900*. Baltimore: Johns Hopkins University Press, 1984.

Turbin, Carole. *Working Women of Collar City: Gender, Class, and Community in Troy, New York, 1864–86*. Urbana: University of Illinois Press, 1992.

Wade, Richard C. *Slavery in the Cities: The South, 1820–1860*. New York: Oxford University Press, 1964.

———. *The Urban Frontier: The Rise of Western Cities, 1790–1830*. Cambridge, MA: Harvard University Press, 1959.

Warner, Sam Bass, Jr. *Streetcar Suburbs: The Process of Growth in Boston, 1870–1900*. New York: Atheneum, 1974.

Wilentz, Sean. *Chants Democratic: New York City and the Rise of the American Working Class, 1788–1850*. New York: Oxford University Press, 1984.

INDEX

ABOUT THE AUTHOR

Ivan D. Steen is a member of the Department of History at the University of Albany, State University of New York, where he directs the graduate program in public history and the oral history program. He has been teaching a popular course on the history of the American city for more than thirty years. In addition to publishing numerous articles and essays in the field of American urban history, he has lectured widely and made television and radio appearances. His current research projects include studies of the New York State Urban Development Corporation under Edward J. Logue and of Albany politics during the long tenure of Mayor Erastus Corning, 2nd.